**GLOBAL**VIEWPOINTS

# Extremism

# Other Books of Related Interest:

## Current Controversies Series

Islamophobia

## Introducing Issues with Opposing Viewpoints Series

The Taliban

## Opposing Viewpoints Series

Anti-Semitism

Dictatorships

Gendercide

**GLOBAL**VIEWPOINTS

# Extremism

*Noël Merino, Book Editor*

**GREENHAVEN PRESS**
*A part of Gale, Cengage Learning*

GALE
CENGAGE Learning·

Farmington Hills, Mich • San Francisco • New York • Waterville, Maine
Meriden, Conn • Mason, Ohio • Chicago

Elizabeth Des Chenes, *Director, Content Strategy*
Douglas Dentino, *Manager, New Product*

© 2014 Greenhaven Press, a part of Gale, Cengage Learning

WCN: 01-100-101

Gale and Greenhaven Press are registered trademarks used herein under license.

*For more information, contact:*
Greenhaven Press
27500 Drake Rd.
Farmington Hills, MI 48331-3535
Or you can visit our Internet site at gale.cengage.com

For product information and technology assistance, contact us at

Gale Customer Support, 1-800-877-4253
For permission to use material from this text or product, submit all requests online at www.cengage.com/permissions

Further permissions questions can be emailed to permissionrequest@cengage.com

Articles in Greenhaven Press anthologies are often edited for length to meet page requirements. In addition, original titles of these works are changed to clearly present the main thesis and to explicitly indicate the author's opinion. Every effort is made to ensure that Greenhaven Press accurately reflects the original intent of the authors. Every effort has been made to trace the owners of copyrighted material.

Cover image copyright © Rachel Megawhat/Demotix/Corbis.

**LIBRARY OF CONGRESS CATALOGING-IN-PUBLICATION DATA**

Extremism / Noël Merino, book editor.
     pages cm. -- (global viewpoints)
     Includes bibliographical references and index.
     ISBN 978-0-7377-6908-1 (hardcover) -- ISBN 978-0-7377-6909-8 (pbk.)
     1. Radicalism--Juvenile literature. I. Merino, Noël.
     HN49.R33E982 2014
     303.48'4--dc23

                                                                    2013047328

Printed in the United States of America
 2 3 4 5 6          18 17 16 15 14

# Contents

## Chapter 1: Extremism Around the World

# Chapter 2: The Causes of Extremism

## Chapter 3: Extremism and Religion

# Chapter 4: Dealing with Extremism

Recent research questions the supposed achievements of de-radicalization programs, suggesting that they may not be helping to reduce extremism.

# Foreword

*"The problems of all of humanity can*
*only be solved by all of humanity."*
*—Swiss author Friedrich Dürrenmatt*

Global interdependence has become an undeniable reality. Mass media and technology have increased worldwide access to information and created a society of global citizens. Understanding and navigating this global community is a challenge, requiring a high degree of information literacy and a new level of learning sophistication.

Building on the success of its flagship series, Opposing Viewpoints, Greenhaven Press has created the Global Viewpoints series to examine a broad range of current, often controversial topics of worldwide importance from a variety of international perspectives. Providing students and other readers with the information they need to explore global connections and think critically about worldwide implications, each Global Viewpoints volume offers a panoramic view of a topic of widespread significance.

Drugs, famine, immigration—a broad, international treatment is essential to do justice to social, environmental, health, and political issues such as these. Junior high, high school, and early college students, as well as general readers, can all use Global Viewpoints anthologies to discern the complexities relating to each issue. Readers will be able to examine unique national perspectives while, at the same time, appreciating the interconnectedness that global priorities bring to all nations and cultures.

Material in each volume is selected from a diverse range of sources, including journals, magazines, newspapers, nonfiction books, speeches, government documents, pamphlets, organization newsletters, and position papers. Global Viewpoints is truly global, with material drawn primarily from international sources available in English and secondarily from US sources with extensive international coverage.

Features of each volume in the Global Viewpoints series include:

- An **annotated table of contents** that provides a brief summary of each essay in the volume, including the name of the country or area covered in the essay.

- An **introduction** specific to the volume topic.

- A **world map** to help readers locate the countries or areas covered in the essays.

- For each viewpoint, an **introduction** that contains notes about the author and source of the viewpoint explains why material from the specific country is being presented, summarizes the main points of the viewpoint, and offers three **guided reading questions** to aid in understanding and comprehension.

- **For further discussion** questions that promote critical thinking by asking the reader to compare and contrast aspects of the viewpoints or draw conclusions about perspectives and arguments.

- A worldwide list of **organizations to contact** for readers seeking additional information.

- A **periodical bibliography** for each chapter and a **bibliography of books** on the volume topic to aid in further research.

- A comprehensive **subject index** to offer access to people, places, events, and subjects cited in the text, with the countries covered in the viewpoints highlighted.

Global Viewpoints is designed for a broad spectrum of readers who want to learn more about current events, history, political science, government, international relations, economics, environmental science, world cultures, and sociology—students doing research for class assignments or debates, teachers and faculty seeking to supplement course materials, and others wanting to understand current issues better. By presenting how people in various countries perceive the root causes, current consequences, and proposed solutions to worldwide challenges, Global Viewpoints volumes offer readers opportunities to enhance their global awareness and their knowledge of cultures worldwide.

# Introduction

*"The labeling of activities, people, and groups as 'extremist,' and the defining of what is 'ordinary' in any setting is always a subjective and political matter."*

—Peter T. Coleman and
Andrea Bartoli, "Addressing Extremism"

The term "extremism" is used to identify radical belief doctrines outside of the mainstream. According to *Merriam-Webster*, extremism is "belief in and support for ideas that are very far from what most people consider correct or reasonable." *Oxford English Dictionary* defines it as "the holding of extreme political or religious views." Thus, the label of "extremist" is always likely to come from the outside. In addition, the definition of extremism will vary across time and cultures, depending on what is deemed to be reasonable.

What sets extremists apart from adherents of more moderate ideologies is often the attempt to bring about change by radical measures. The *American Heritage Dictionary* defines an "extremist" as "a person who advocates or resorts to measures beyond the norm, especially in politics." *Oxford English Dictionary* notes that an extremist is a person who not only holds extreme views, but also especially "resorts to or advocates extreme action." These actions by extremists to bring about change may involve social protest, the attempt to dismantle the existing political structure, and frequently may involve violence. Thus, there is often a link between extremism and terrorism.

Extremism can be found worldwide and among all ethnicities, religions, and ways of life. What distinguishes extremists from others is their distance from the mainstream. Extremism is often associated with religion and, since the

September 11, 2001, terrorist attacks on the United States, frequently associated with terrorism and Islamists. Yet, extremism is possible within all religions. As former prime minister of Norway Kjell Magne Bondevik noted:

> All religions can be misused by extremists who are seeking to find arguments for persecution or a holy war. History has shown it again and again. We have seen it in Christianity, in the form of the Medieval Crusades, and the persecution of non-Christians and heretics right up to our own times. I am thinking for instance of the so-called "Army of God" in the US which condones the killing of medical personnel who are involved in abortions.
>
> We have seen it in Judaism; the very expression "zealot" comes from a group of Jews who used assassination in their fight against the Romans and the Romanization of the Jews. And we see it today in the form of groups such as Khatz, and Chanitri.
>
> And we have seen it in Islam. The word "assassin" comes from an extremist Muslim sect of the 11th century, which used murder as a tool in their fight against the crusaders and mainstream Muslim leaders. Today al Qaeda is the most prominent example of terrorists who misuse Islam. But we have also seen by terrorists of other religions in places like India and Japan.[1]

The *New York Times* reported in June 2013 that violent extremism was flourishing among a group of Buddhist monks, usually known for their nonviolence, in Myanmar who are spreading anti-Muslim sentiment, which has resulted in the death and displacement of Muslims by lynch mobs.

Extremism is not always associated with religion, however, and is frequently constituted by radical political beliefs. Ex-

---

1. Kjell Magne Bondevik, "Religion and Religious Extremism," International Summit on Democracy, Terrorism, and Security, March 10, 2005. http://summit.clubmadrid.org/keynotes/religion-and-religious-extremism.html.

tremists are feared not only for violence, but also because of their desire to upend political structures and implement their views forcefully. Matthew Goodwin, a lecturer in politics in the School of Politics and International Relations at the University of Nottingham and an associate fellow of Chatham House, claims that extremist political parties are gaining ground in several European countries, advancing their message and policies through democratic channels. Goodwin says that the populist extremist parties in Europe "are an ideologically motivated group guided by clear political goals: they are profoundly concerned about immigration and rising ethnic and cultural diversity, and they feel threatened by immigrants and Muslims."[2] He claims that such political parties are extremist because of two core features: "they reject the principle of human equality, and hence advocate exclusionary policies towards immigrants and minority groups; and they adhere to a populist anti-establishment strategy that is deeply critical of the mainstream parties and is ambiguous if not hostile towards liberal representative democracy."

Labeling a group or individual extremist is usually a pejorative connotation that expresses disapproval. Thus, there is often disagreement about what political groups ought to be labeled "extremist." In fact, labeling a group or individual extremist is sometimes a political tactic used to undermine the legitimacy of the group or call into question an ideology. *National Review Online* editor-at-large Jonah Goldberg claims that in American politics a double standard is used when applying the term. He says, "'Extreme' is a funny word these days. It's often used by mainstream news outlets to describe the tea parties and the tea-party-friendly caucus in the GOP."[3] However, he claims that members of the Occupy Wall Street

2. Matthew Goodwin, "Right Response: Understanding and Countering Populist Extremism in Europe," Chatham House, September 2011.
3. Jonah Goldberg, "Sorting Out the 'Extremists,'" *National Review Online*, October 7, 2011.

movement are not deemed extremists even when the communications director of the movement said his goal was to overthrow the government.

Perceptions about extremism and responses to it vary around the world. There is much debate about the causes of extremism and its connection with religion. Additionally, what works to alleviate extremism in one part of the world may not be effective elsewhere. Shedding light on this ongoing debate, various viewpoints from around the world regarding the issue of extremism, its causes, and its solutions are explored in *Global Viewpoints: Extremism.*

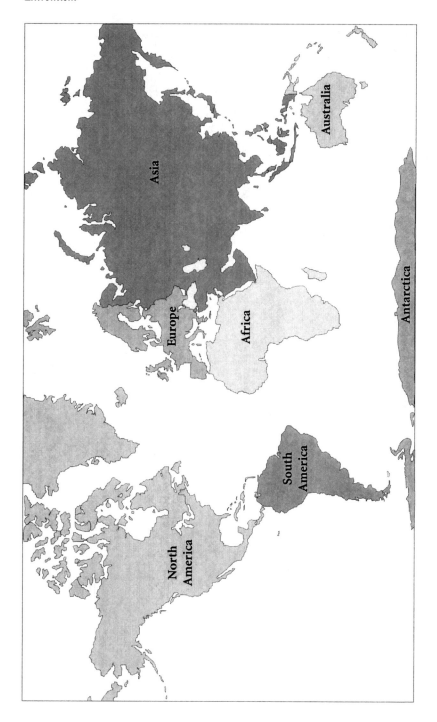

 **GLOBAL**VIEWPOINTS

# Extremism Around the World

# In Tunisia and Egypt, Islamist Groups Are Becoming Less Extreme

*Noman Benotman and Hayden Pirkle*

*In the following viewpoint, Noman Benotman and Hayden Pirkle argue that the political pragmatism of Hizb al-Nahda in Tunisia and the Muslim Brotherhood in Egypt illustrates why the two Islamist groups have public support. Despite criticism of the West, the authors claim that dependency on Western aid will continue to temper radicalism. Benotman is the former head of the Libyan militant organization known as the Libyan Islamic Fighting Group. Pirkle is a research intern at the Quilliam Foundation, a London-based counter-extremism organization.*

As you read, consider the following questions:

1. According to the authors, Hizb al-Nahda was banned in Tunisia until what year?

2. Egypt's Ikhwan movement moderated its message during what decade, according to Benotman and Pirkle?

3. According to the authors, Tunisia is believed to have received how much in loans and grants from various European Union institutions between 2011 and 2013?

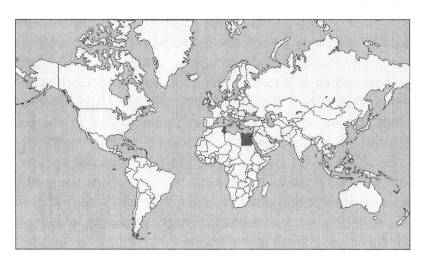

The Middle Eastern uprisings beginning at the end of 2010 in Tunisia and spreading throughout much of the Arab world in 2011, deposed several of the region's longtime autocrats. Having already resulted in a shift in the political paradigm of much of the region, this phenomenon, known globally as the "Arab Spring", continues on today. The first dominoes to fall in the Arab uprisings—Tunisia and Egypt—have now seen democratically elected mainstream Islamist groups replacing their ousted dictators, marking the transition of Tunisia's Hizb al-Nahda and Egypt's Muslim Brotherhood from a historic opposition position to that of an official political power. Undoubtedly, this transition carries considerable political, economic, and social implications not only for the region but also for the wider global community. It is therefore important to understand the history of these Islamist groups and what they stand for so that we can begin to understand how and why they were able to gain public support and come into power democratically.

## Hizb al-Nahda and the Muslim Brotherhood

In 1981 during the aftermath of the Iranian Revolution, Rachid Ghannouchi founded the Movement of the Islamic

Tendency, which in 1988 became 'Hizb al-Nahda'. A year later in 1989, Islamists from Hizb al-Nahda, running as independents in Tunisian national elections, finished second to Zine El Abidine Ben Ali's ruling party with some 17 per cent of the vote. In response, Ben Ali instantly banned Hizb al-Nahda from Tunisia and its founder Ghannouchi fled to the UK [United Kingdom] to avoid persecution. Hizb al-Nahda remained banned in Tunisia until 2011, when the interim government that replaced the Ben Ali regime legalised the group. Rachid Ghannouchi soon returned from self-imposed exile declaring that he would not run for election, but would remain Hizb al-Nahda's ideological leader.

---

*The first dominoes to fall in the Arab uprisings—Tunisia and Egypt—have now seen democratically elected mainstream Islamist groups replacing their ousted dictators.*

---

Egypt's Muslim Brotherhood movement, also known as the Ikhwan, shares a similar albeit longer history to its Tunisian counterpart. Founded by Hassan al-Banna in 1928, the Muslim Brotherhood has spread beyond Egyptian borders and become one of the world's largest Islamist organisations. Despite its size however, the Brotherhood has for almost all of its history been forced into the ranks of illegal opposition, being first banned by the Egyptian monarchy in 1949. In 1952, the Ikhwan saw an opportunity to enter mainstream politics following a coup overthrowing the monarchy by the Free Officers, a group which was originally sympathetic with the Muslim Brotherhood movement. Two years later the Free Officers, led by Gamal Abdel Nasser, banned the Ikhwan following a suspected Brotherhood-orchestrated assassination attempt against Nasser's life. This crackdown ensured that the Ikhwan's Islamist ideology was unable to replace the ideology of Arab socialism which permeated the region for the following 20 and more years. From 1954 until the aftermath of the Arab

Spring, the Ikhwan's status of opposition has been rather confused, with it being tolerated by the Egyptian state to varying degrees at varying times.

## The Idea of Shari'ah as Law

Whilst both the Muslim Brotherhood and Hizb al-Nahda are considered by many to be relatively moderate Islamist movements, their ideologies have historically been based on the establishment of their idea of shari'ah as law by necessity. Hizb al-Nahda's founder prescribes for Muslims to never stop striving for the implementation of a version of Islam in government based on what they see as shari'ah. Despite this, however, Ghannouchi advocates temporary alliances with other, non-Islamist parties within the Tunisian political spectrum exhibiting the rhetorical and political pragmatism which currently characterizes Hizb al-Nahda. This stance of cooperating with non-Islamist parties has provoked anger among Tunisia's hard-line Salafist groups, who believe that Hizb al-Nahda is overly compromising and too lenient politically.

> In the lead-up to the events of 2011 . . . both groups gained popular legitimacy, undermining the incumbent regimes in Tunisia and Egypt and advocating anti-Western rhetoric and attitudes.

In 1940, al-Banna (the founder and ideological leader of the Muslim Brotherhood), made the Ikhwan's political intentions clear, declaring that the group 'does not recognize any governmental order that does not focus in its essence on Islam or derive from it, and we do not recognize these political parties or these traditional forms that the infidels, the enemies of Islam forced us to rule by . . . and we will work for the revival of the Islamic order of rule in all its facets and the establishment of an Islamic government in this order.' During the 1990s, however, this discourse was moderated in response to accusations from secularists and other non-Islamists that the Ikhwan were attempting to establish a repressive theocratic state. Since moderating [its] message, the Brotherhood [has] been publicising [its] desire for Egypt to establish and maintain a civil state with an "Islamic reference", rather than become a full-blown Islamist state. However, some critics speculate that the Brotherhood only moderated its political ambitions to appease the then incumbent regime of Hosni Mubarak and other oppositional forces, and the group will reverse this moderation when the moment is right. Others believe that the moderation of the Brotherhood's discourse is indicative of [its] adaptation to the realities of the current political system.

## Attitudes Towards the West

In the lead-up to the events of 2011, which thrust Hizb al-Nahda and the Muslim Brotherhood from the shadows of opposition to the fore of mainstream politics, both groups gained popular legitimacy, undermining the incumbent regimes in Tunisia and Egypt and advocating anti-Western rhetoric and attitudes. Such criticism, especially towards the United States and Israel, serves to legitimise the viewpoints of Islamist groups, including the Muslim Brotherhood and Hizb al-Nahda. However, despite being highly critical of Western secularism, 'imperialism', and the West's historic support of undemocratic regimes (which is viewed as hypocritical to the ideals and values of the West), Hizb al-Nahda's Ghannouchi seems to hold ideals of democracy in high regard.

The Muslim Brotherhood's criticism of the West is less pragmatic and insightful than its Tunisian counterpart's. It includes the stereotypical condemnation of Western imperialism and decadence, and at times, has been rather alarming. Perhaps the most notable case of this rhetoric is the much-publicised case of current Egyptian Muslim Brotherhood president Mohammed Morsi who denigrated Zionists, lashed

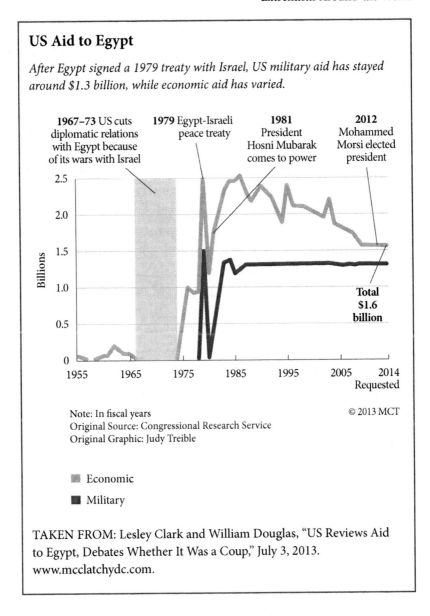

## US Aid to Egypt

*After Egypt signed a 1979 treaty with Israel, US military aid has stayed around $1.3 billion, while economic aid has varied.*

**1967–73** US cuts diplomatic relations with Egypt because of its wars with Israel

**1979** Egypt-Israeli peace treaty

**1981** President Hosni Mubarak comes to power

**2012** Mohammed Morsi elected president

Total $1.6 billion

Note: In fiscal years
Original Source: Congressional Research Service
Original Graphic: Judy Treible

© 2013 MCT

Economic

Military

TAKEN FROM: Lesley Clark and William Douglas, "US Reviews Aid to Egypt, Debates Whether It Was a Coup," July 3, 2013. www.mcclatchydc.com.

out at the United States and European actors for being so-called Zionist "supporters", and called Barack Obama a liar. Despite pressure from the United States in January [2013] to repudiate his past comments, there has been nothing but silence on the matter from Morsi and the Muslim Brotherhood.

# The Future of Tunisia, Egypt and the West

It is important to remember that there is a considerable difference between rhetoric and action—now in power, both Hizb al-Nahda and the Muslim Brotherhood are faced with the alarming realities of high-stakes politics, resulting in them having to adopt a willingness to cooperate and engage with the international community, much to the discontent of hardline Salafist and jihadist groups in Tunisia and Egypt. Despite criticism from their more radical counterparts, this willingness to cooperate is necessary for Hizb al-Nahda and the Muslim Brotherhood because of the economic and political realities which have presented themselves in both countries.

*Both Hizb al-Nahda and the Muslim Brotherhood are unlikely, any time soon, to act on their disapproval of Western cultures and practices.*

Since 2011, the US has provided approximately $320 million to Tunisia, which is believed to have also received €4 billion in loans and grants from various European Union institutions between 2011 and 2013. Similarly, Egypt, which faces increasingly dire economic conditions, receives American military and economic support, which over the past 33 years has averaged some $2 billion annually. Egypt also maintains considerable trade relations (mostly textiles) with Israel—any attempts to break this peace agreement with Israel would result in a cancellation of American military and economic aid.

In short, both Tunisia and Egypt are, for the time being, heavily dependent on Western aid and loans. More importantly they rely on Western political support and assistance to bring about development. For now, this means that the Islamist nature of Hizb al-Nahda and the Muslim Brotherhood is not likely to hinder collaborative working with the international community on strategic issues in the Middle East region. Therefore, both Hizb al-Nahda and the Muslim Brotherhood are unlikely, any time soon, to act on their disapproval of Western cultures and practices, biting the hands that feed them and jeopardising the much-needed resources that the West provides.

# In the Sahel and Horn of Africa, Islamic Militancy Is Increasing

*Terje Østebø*

*In the following viewpoint, Terje Østebø argues that the rise of Islamic militant movements in parts of Africa poses a threat to stability. Nonetheless, Østebø claims that the movements are largely focused on local concerns and do not possess great military power. Østebø cautions that ill-considered interventions can reinforce the narrative of the militants, inadvertently leading to recruitment, especially among the disenfranchised youth of the region. Østebø is an assistant professor in the Department of Religion and the Center for African Studies at the University of Florida.*

As you read, consider the following questions:

1. According to Østebø, Islamic militancy first surfaced in Somalia in what decade?
2. What is Salafism, according to the author?
3. What does the author identify as a recurrent problem in less democratic regimes, such as Ethiopia and Uganda?

Terje Østebø, "Islamic Militancy in Africa," *Africa Security Brief*, no. 23, Africa Center for Strategic Studies, November 2012, pp. 1–6. Copyright © 2012 by Africa Center for Strategic Studies. All rights reserved. Reproduced by permission.

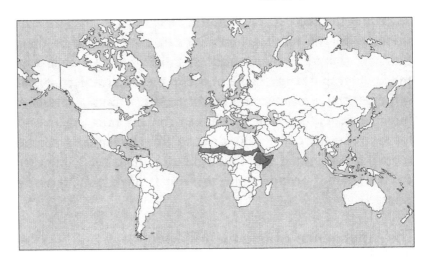

The seizure of more than half of Mali's land area by Islamic militants, the growing violence of Boko Haram in northern Nigeria, and years of religious-inspired violence in Somalia have heightened attention on Islamic militancy in Africa. In the process, violent clashes between insurgent groups and governments in the Sahel and the Horn of Africa have increased, the armed capacity of militant organizations has expanded, terrorist attacks against civilians including suicide bombings have escalated, militants' strict moral codes—enforced through stoning and amputation—have been imposed, sacred historical sites have been destroyed, and hundreds of thousands of civilians have been displaced. Militants' ability to seize and control vast territory for extended periods of time has prolonged and obstructed the process of state-building in Somalia, while in Mali it has severed the northern from the southern half of the country and exacerbated a political impasse in Bamako. Protracted instability in parts of the Sahara-Sahel, furthermore, has the potential to ripple throughout the region. The prospect of the emergence of Islamic militancy and the escalation of tensions elsewhere on the continent is likewise a cause for concern.

While the risks of escalation are significant, the gains of these Islamic militant groups are not attributable to their military strength. Rather, their expanded influence is just as much a symptom of fragile and complex political contexts. More generally, Islamic militancy in Africa today represents the intersection of broader trends in contemporary Islam and local circumstances. Responding to the challenge is all the more difficult in that very little is known about these often secretive Islamic groups, some of which have only recently emerged.

## The Emergence of Islamic Militancy in Africa

Islamic militancy is understood here as Muslim groups and movements that, based on religious preferences, seek to enforce religious, social, and political norms through violence. Religious preferences are in turn defined as scriptural-based interpretations viewed by the actors as authoritative. Islamic militancy is, in other words, different from Islamic movements that seek political change through nonviolent means or to promote reforms of a religious nature—through, for example, education and *da'wah* (proselytizing). It should also be noted that Islamic militancy reflects a minority perspective within the spectrum of Islamic ideologies.

---

*While the risks of escalation are significant, the gains of these Islamic militant groups are not attributable to their military strength.*

---

Islamic militancy in Somalia first surfaced in the mid-1980s with the formation of al Itihaad al Islamiya ("Islamic Unity"), which expanded its military operations in the early 1990s. Al Itihaad disappeared from the scene after 1996, yet its ideas and main actors continued to play roles in the highly diverse [Union of] Islamic Courts (UIC) movement that emerged in the mid-2000s. In 2006, the UIC managed to secure control over Mogadishu for some months before being crushed by the Ethiopian intervention in December of that year. This subsequently gave rise to al-Shabaab, which represented a new generation of Islamic militants ever more determined to use violent action to achieve their goals. In addition to waging a guerilla war that enabled it to gain control over large areas of southern Somalia, al-Shabaab added suicide bombing to its repertoire. Several offensives by the African Union Mission in Somalia (AMISOM) and Somali government troops since 2011, later joined by Kenyan and Ethiopian forces, dramatically weakened al-Shabaab's capacity.

Recent activities by the group popularly known as Boko Haram (*Boko* meaning "Western, secular education" in Hausa, and *Haram* meaning "sinful" in Arabic) have spurred renewed attention to Islamic militancy in Nigeria. The group was established around 2002 by Mohammed Yusuf, a self-educated activist, inspired by the Islamist Muslim Students' Society of Nigeria (MSSN), formed in 1954, and in particular Ibrahim al Zakzaky, as well as by the Salafi scholar Ja'afar Mahmud Adam. Yusuf eventually embarked on his own ideological path, distinct from mainstream Islamists and Salafis in Nigeria. Yusuf was actively involved in the enforcement of the shari'a laws introduced in northern Nigeria in the early 2000s, yet soon felt that the process was too accommodating. While Boko Haram repeatedly clashed with Nigerian security forces in a low-intensity conflict beginning in 2003, the violence intensified, following a brief lull, after Yusuf was killed by Nigerian police in 2009. It gained worldwide attention with the suicide bombing of the United Nations' Nigerian headquarters in Abuja in August 2011, which was followed by attacks on police stations and Christian churches in subsequent years. Boko Haram's leadership structure since Yusuf's death remains unclear, yet the group has demonstrated both the will and capacity to escalate its insurgent activities.

The two main Islamic militant movements operating in northern Mali are Ansar al-Din ("Defenders of the Faith") and Jama'at Tawhid Wal Jihad fi Garbi Afriqqiya ("Movement for Unity and Jihad in West Africa," or MUJWA). Ansar al-Din was formed at the end of 2011 by Iyad Ag Ghali, a former Tuareg rebel leader, who is often described as a pragmatic opportunist. MUJWA was created around the same time but very little is known about the group except for its stated objectives of waging jihad in West Africa and that it seems to be heavily funded by drug trafficking and kidnapping for ransom. The rank and file are mostly Tuaregs, Mauritanian and Malian Arabs, as well as sympathizers from Nigeria and other Sahelian countries. Both Ansar al-Din and MUJWA surfaced during fighting launched in January 2012 by the National Movement for the Liberation of Azawad (MNLA), a nationalist and self-declared secular movement struggling for an independent Tuareg homeland. Previously fighting in loose association, the relationship between MNLA and the Islamic militants became increasingly strained in May 2012, with the latter outmaneuvering and, in some areas, clashing with the MNLA to assume control over strategic towns in northern Mali. There has been much speculation about internal disagreements between MUJWA, Ansar al-Din, and the foreign-led and better known al Qaeda in the Islamic Maghreb (AQIM). This may be due to ideological disagreements, personality clashes, ethnic differences, or the control over the extensive smuggling networks in the Sahel and Sahara. Accordingly, the military and political strength of the Sahelian Islamic militant groups and the viability of a coherent al Qaeda–like front in this region remain questionable.

## The Militant Movements' Ideological Features

While political and socioeconomic factors are important, the very fact that these movements define themselves in *religious* terms makes it imperative to recognize their ideological content. Islamic militancy in Africa is part of a broader, global ideological current. In some cases, this includes links to like-minded organizations outside Africa. Unfortunately, the lack of thorough investigations of such connections often reduces the complexity of such ideological bonds to the diffuse notion of "global Islam." In fact, contemporary Islam is characterized by increased doctrinal heterogeneity and fragmentation, which inevitably impact the on-the-ground actions of Islamic militants. Groups feature a high degree of selective interpretations of religious tenets, particular local appropriations, and a lack of ideological coherence that propel them on multiple potential trajectories that can be difficult to chart.

*The very fact that these movements define themselves in* religious *terms makes it imperative to recognize their ideological content.*

Recognizing the variations, current Islamic militancy in Africa can best be characterized as Salafi militancy. Salafism is at the outset a religious movement—usually nonviolent—devoted to the struggle for religious purity, personal piety, and Islamic morality. This has largely centered on combating local cultural and Sufi elements in Islam. Since the 1980s, it has also actively resisted Western influences—seen as negatively affecting Muslims' religiosity. Both al-Shabaab and Boko Haram have their roots in Salafi movements that surfaced in Somalia and Nigeria in the 1970s. Salafism, together with Jama'at al-Tabligh (a worldwide nonviolent Islamic propagation movement), started making significant impacts in central and northern Mali in the early 1990s, represented by various Islamic NGOs [nongovernmental organizations], da'wah activities, and religious schools. The leader of Ansar al-Din, Iyad Ag Ghali, became a Tabligh adherent in the early 2000s before gradually turning in a more militant direction. His stay in Saudi Arabia as a member of Mali's diplomatic mission prob-

33

ably brought him into contact with militant Salafi teachings, which gradually shaped his jihadi thinking.

Salafism has always had an ambiguous view of politics and political power. In general, it has held a rather xenophobic attitude, fearing that political engagement would compel Salafis to cooperate with secularists and non-Salafis, threatening their religious purity. While Salafis in principle favor the establishment of an Islamic state, their political ideology for doing so has not been well defined and they have instead usually devoted themselves to da'wah and teaching their religious precepts. The general argument is that Islamization of society from below would be the requisite precursor for establishing an Islamic political order. Such notions were clearly noticeable in Boko Haram's early phase, as it was opposed to Western education and argued for severing any connections to the secular state. Emblematic of Salafi xenophobia, the group's retreat to Kannamma in 2003, a small town on the border of Niger, represented a withdrawal from "defiled" space and a form of *hijra* ("refuge") to maintain religious purity.

In recent decades, trends within Salafism have increasingly called for the establishment of an Islamic political order to achieve its quest for religious purity. This is a result of growing influences from Muslim Brotherhood ideology—particularly from Sayyid Qutb, one of the Egyptian Muslim Brotherhood's main ideologues. His teachings, which emphasized political engagement, paved the way for further elaborations on the relationships between purity, armed struggle, and political power. These influences are clearly visible within al-Shabaab, Sahelian militants, and Boko Haram. Specifically, there is the perception that Islam is threatened by contaminating forces, that religious purity is impossible to maintain under non-Islamic political systems, and that the use of violent force is the only recourse. However fragile, both al-Shabaab and Malian militants have managed to secure territorial control toward this end. Through the establishment of strict regulations aimed at creating a pious environment, they have destroyed Sufi shrines and curbed "immoral" activities such as smoking, drinking alcohol, and chewing khat through the application of *hudud* ("restriction") penalties such as capital punishment, amputation, or flogging. Boko Haram, which has not managed to secure similar territorial control, advocates an identical program of politicized purity—to be imposed on all Nigerians regardless of religious affiliation. Parallel to the expansion of Salafism in Nigeria, a more assertive political Islamism was promoted by the MSSN. This movement was inspired by resurgent Islamist thinking during the 1970s and by the Iranian Revolution in 1979, and gained much support among Nigeria's Muslim youth. Neither the Salafis of this time nor the MSSN, however, were engaged in any form of organized violent political activism.

## A Homegrown Phenomenon

While African Islamic militancy remains interlinked with broader ideological currents, it is clear that circumstances in local contexts have been important catalysts for its emergence and trajectory. These are largely homegrown phenomena, wherein individual Islamic militant groups emerge and evolve from local concerns, are created and run by locally situated actors, and have an agenda that focuses on the immediate context.

The Malian government's failure to consistently invest and maintain a strong state presence in the north, for example, created an enabling environment for the expansion of Islamic militancy and the escalation of violence in this region. Notably, it was local militant Islamists, rather than AQIM, that were behind this escalation and routing of the government forces and MNLA. Similarly, indications are that these militant groups are more concerned with supplanting presumed corrupt regimes and establishing Islamic rule in the local contexts the militants control than waging a broad global jihad as advocated by AQIM.

35

In the same way, the unique political history of Somalia remains important for understanding current developments. Years of authoritarian rule under Siad Barre produced democratic deficits and a weak civil society. As the country collapsed into civil war in the early 1990s, the door was wide open for a range of groups to continually fight one another in a scramble for power and resources. What few observers noticed was that Somalis responded to the violent havoc by flocking to their mosques, finding refuge in religion. This was an important precursor for the gradual politicization of Islam in Somalia. To varying degrees, both the UIC's and al-Shabaab's struggle for the implementation of Islamic law was aimed at ending the anarchic violence and establishing political stability.

---

*These are largely homegrown phenomena, wherein individual Islamic militant groups emerge and evolve from local concerns.*

---

Nigeria's distinctive history is also relevant for understanding Boko Haram's program. In particular is the legacy of the Sokoto Caliphate—established by Usman dan Fodio after his famous jihad in the early 19th century—and the experience with British colonialism. The caliphate has on several occasions and in different manners been recognized as a source of pride and a historical reference point for those contesting the secular Nigerian state and arguing for the implementation of Islamic law. This was the case for Mohammed Yusuf's involvement in instituting shari'a in Nigeria's northern states in 2000. Boko Haram's aversion to Western education, moreover, is rooted in the colonial period when secular schools run by Christian missionaries emerged. Muslims in the north already had their structures of Islamic teaching and were reluctant to send their children to the new Christian schools. The fear that such secular education would lead students away from Islam is now being revived in Boko Haram's calls for boycotts.

---

*Indiscriminate action to combat Islamic militancy could*
*. . . radicalize a local context and lead to escalation.*

---

## The Importance of Local Context

Another important and often overlooked factor is ethnicity. While the MNLA has an explicit ethno-nationalist identity, the other Islamic militant groups in Mali have their own ethnic constituencies, including Sahelian Arabs and Tuareg subclans. For instance, there are claims that ethnic boundaries are complicating relations between the Malian militants and the Algerian-dominated AQIM. The former's objective of establishing an Islamic state may be less expansive and could remain confined within territories defined by ethnicity. Islamic militancy in Somalia is similarly connected to Somali nationalism, which in turn is related to regional politics. UIC's high-profile declaration of jihad against Ethiopia in 2006 had a clear ethno-nationalist character, stating that "we will leave no stone unturned to integrate our Somali brothers in Kenya and Ethiopia and restore their freedom to live with their ancestors in Somalia." For al-Shabaab, then, the notions of an Islamic state and the Somali nation dovetail and are perceived to be threatened by "infidel" neighboring powers.

Indiscriminate action to combat Islamic militancy could also radicalize a local context and lead to escalation. Blanket labeling of all Islamic movements as militant coupled with unsophisticated and repressive measures risk generating a deeper discontent that could translate into violence. A recurrent problem has been that less democratic regimes, such as Ethiopia and Uganda, issue "anti-terror" legislation to crack down on a range of opposition groups. Meanwhile, Western attempts to combat terror have shown little understanding of local dynamics. If movements without any political agenda or any disposition for militant activism are targeted, local support for militancy could easily escalate. The broad-brush branding of UIC as an Islamic militant threat, leading to the Ethiopian intervention in 2006, was crucial for paving the way for the emergence of al-Shabaab and for further radicalizing developments in Somalia. Therefore, responses to Islamic militancy in Somalia, Nigeria, and northern Mali or in other African contexts where the challenge is less advanced should be considered carefully so as not to exacerbate the situation.

Conflicts also tend to take on a life of their own. Accordingly, repressive measures from political regimes or external actors could bring Islamic militants to fight for their very existence, intensifying violence. Such measures could, at the same time, serve to confirm views on the illegitimacy of the state, adding fuel to an insurgency fire. In the case of Boko Haram, the accelerating conflict with the Nigerian police and security forces has led to an expansion of Boko Haram's objectives and tactics. The quest for revenge after the killing of Mohammed Yusuf and anger over the police's alleged abuse of force in its dealings with Boko Haram members have been important drivers in the escalation of the conflict.

---

*While the rank and file of Islamic militant movements may be socially mixed, a noticeable commonality is the strong presence of youth.*

---

## The Strong Presence of Youth

The emergence of contemporary Islamic movements, both violent and nonviolent, has often been seen as a response to prevailing poverty, unemployment, and socioeconomic deprivation. While economic and social factors clearly are relevant, they remain insufficient for explaining such a complex phenomenon. While such organizations draw many of their members from among the poor, militant messages are typically rejected by the vast majority of the downtrodden. At the same time, Islamic militants attract some supporters from the middle class and the affluent, including professional organizations and study groups organized at universities.

While the rank and file of Islamic militant movements may be socially mixed, a noticeable commonality is the strong presence of youth. This would at the outset fit the thesis of socioeconomic deprivation, as youth constitute the demographic group suffering most from unemployment and bleak economic prospects. African youth, moreover, are not only marginalized economically, but [also are] often alienated from their cultural contexts and burdened by questions of identity and belonging. Contacts with Salafi or Islamist groups and exposure to charismatic leaders, such as Boko Haram's Mohammed Yusuf, frame this alienation in religious terms, in which Islam is presented as the all-encompassing, powerful, and only solution. Both local circumstances and global events are presented as evidence of a world threatening Islam and contradicting the will of God. In addition to being the only option for salvation, membership in Salafi or Islamist movements— whether militant or nonmilitant—also represents a source of empowerment. These groups may not bring an end to poverty or provide jobs, but they give disgruntled youth an alternative universal model for belonging and for social action in which disillusion is exchanged for dignity and marginalization with meaning. Moreover, the emphasis on purity and morality, coupled with the notion of an exclusive access to the truth, generates attitudes of superiority. This, in turn, produces rigid boundaries toward those on the opposite side. "Others" are seen both as threats to religious purity and as targets for expansionist activities. When such thinking is cultivated in tight-knit groups with strong leaders, the road to militancy and violence can easily be a short one.

# In Indonesia, Radicalization in Schools and Prisons Breeds Terrorists

## Michael Bachelard

*In the following viewpoint, Michael Bachelard argues that prisons in Indonesia have become a breeding ground for terrorists, and there are also concerns about terrorist recruitment in boarding schools. Bachelard contends that although law enforcement has cracked down on radicalization, Indonesia cannot keep up with the new radicals being created every day. He claims that the current programs designed to combat extremism are inadequate. Bachelard is the Indonesia correspondent for the* Age *and the* Sydney Morning Herald.

As you read, consider the following questions:

1. In the ten years since the Bali terrorist attacks, the author contends that Indonesia has arrested how many people for terrorism?

2. According to the author, an existing program to combat radicalization in Indonesian prisons applies what three strategies?

3. The author cites an Indonesian psychologist who claims that a private de-radicalization program in the Afghan Alumni Forum has what success rate?

Michael Bachelard, "J Is for Jihad," *Sydney Morning Herald* (Australia), October 7, 2012. www.smh.com.au. Reproduced by permission.

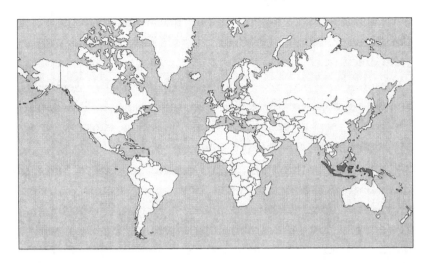

In March this year [2012], a group of Islamist radicals were scoping out new targets in Bali, hoping to enact their own murderous 10th anniversary of the 2002 attacks.

They had surveyed the Hard Rock Cafe in downtown Kuta and the Australian-run La Vida Loca bar in Seminyak. They had chosen a suicide bomber and planned to fund the operation by robbing a money changer and a gold store.

## A Breeding Ground for Terrorists

What is not widely known is that three of the five plotters for "Bali III"—including their leader Hilman, aka Surya—were low-level drug pushers who were radicalised in Kerobokan prison when they were locked up with the original Bali bombers in the early 2000s.

According to research by the International Crisis Group, Hilman, who was serving a seven-year sentence for marijuana possession, was the prisoners' mosque functionary who came under the influence of Bali bomber Imam Samudra. On leaving prison he became a full-time jihadist. Another plotter shared a cell with another Bali bomber, Amrozi.

The radicalisation of their cell mates was the Bali bombers' slow-burn revenge. If an attack had overshadowed this week's

10th anniversary commemoration, they would have their last, posthumous, laugh over their jailers. (Samudra and Amrozi were executed in 2008.)

Indonesia's prisons are a breeding ground for terrorists, and so are some of the Islamic boarding schools. But despite the ever-present threat of terrorism, the Indonesian state shows little interest in tackling this issue.

After the authoritarian and secular regime of Suharto [president of Indonesia] fell in 1998, many groups that were previously repressed thrived under "Reformasi"—Indonesia's flowering of freedom. Among them were those groups with a radical religious agenda who wanted to replace the state of Indonesia entirely with a caliphate under Islamic law.

## A Crackdown on Radicalism

Until the Bali bombings, whose death toll of 202 woke it from its torpor, the newly democratic Indonesia knew little or nothing of the growing number of deadly men in its midst.

Ten years on, Indonesian law enforcement, spearheaded by Detachment 88, the anti-terrorist police, has had great success in cracking down on religiously inspired radicalism. On his recent visit to Indonesia, Australian Defence Minister Stephen Smith lavished praise, saying: "There is no country in the world that is more successful in arresting and prosecuting terrorists."

---

*Indonesia's prisons are a breeding ground for terrorists, and so are some of the Islamic boarding schools.*

---

Since the first Bali attack, Indonesia has arrested 700 people for terrorism offences and prosecuted 500. For every 10 prosecuted, another one suspected terrorist—including some of Asia's most dangerous men—has been killed by police on the streets.

That success story, though, contains the frightening truth that, in 10 years, Indonesia has produced 500 people with a proven link to terror, and many more who have gone unnoticed so far.

Every few months a new plot, with a new set of plotters, is uncovered. Some, such as a recent group calling itself "al-Qaeda Indonesia", have progressed far enough to start making bombs—albeit ones which blew up by accident in the kitchen.

Many now believe that law enforcement alone is not enough. They say the country's jihad factories, which still pump out recruits, must be shut down and the radicals de-radicalised. The effort so far, though, has been piecemeal and anaemic, marred by poor funding and follow-through and an apparent lack of political will.

## Hardened Jihadis in Prison

In Indonesian prisons, extremist preachers, terrorists and would-be jihadists are locked up with common criminals. Low-level terrorists—youngsters or those who have dabbled around the edges of a radical group—are housed with hardened jihadis, persuasive men with a seductive story to tell.

The most infamous of these men, Abu Bakar Bashir, is serving a 15-year sentence for helping set up a paramilitary training camp in Aceh in 2010. But inside he is still surrounded by acolytes and young prisoners, and boasts in a written interview with the *Sunday Age* that he is "busy spreading the word of Allah to the people".

His words remain unrepentantly full of violent jihad—ideas of noble martyrdom and the overthrow of the state of Indonesia so "that people's life may be managed by Allah's law". Bashir refers repeatedly to "evil Indonesia" and offers up a contradictory mishmash of arguments to explain and justify the Bali bombs.

First, he asserts that the massive bombs were set by three individuals, "Mukhlas and his two friends". He calls them "mujahideen [holy warriors] who actively defended Islam" and were "slaughtered by the Jews, the United States and their allies".

---

*In Indonesian prisons, extremist preachers, terrorists and would-be jihadists are locked up with common criminals.*

---

In the very next paragraph he claims the bombs were part of a conspiracy, a "micro-nuclear device" planted by the US to discredit Islam. "So it was the US who essentially killed tens of Australians, not the three mujahideen," he writes. "God willing, Islam will win due to Allah's help of jihad," he writes, before exhorting Australian journalists to "convert to Islam so you will be saved".

Ask most ordinary Indonesians about Bashir and his ilk and they shake their heads and pronounce him "gila"—"crazy". But his carefully cultivated look of a gentle and wise old scholar has made his loony rhetoric surprisingly resilient, despite the patent failure of the populace of Indonesia to rise up in support of holy war after the Bali bombings.

Jemaah Islamiah, Bashir's former terror vehicle, is now mistrusted in the radical community because a few of its high-profile members—notably Bali bomber Ali Imron, and former senior member Nasir Abbas—"turned" and offered information to police. But a whole slew of new followers have emerged. Bashir's new radical group, Jemaah Ansharut Tauhid, or JAT, has been involved in many of the latter-day plots that police have uncovered.

## The Teaching of Jihad

As disturbing is the fact that the Ngruki boarding school Bashir co-founded, and where his son (and leader of JAT) Abdul Rohim is a teacher, is still pumping out fresh-faced "martyrs". Bali bomber Idris, an old boy of Ngruki, said of his alma mater recently: "That is where jihad was taught." But suggest that the school in Ngruki, a suburb of Solo, might be closed down, and Indonesians simply laugh.

All schools look something alike, and, apart from the enormous mosque being built and the separate sections for boys and girls, al-Mukmin school in suburban Ngruki is no exception. The classrooms have whiteboards and teachers at the front, and rowdy students in rows. In science the boys are learning about microbes. Graffiti and motivational posters adorn the walls.

But in the girls' section, along with exhortations to pious (veiled) womanhood, is a notice board. Pinned to it is a graphic photograph of a dead man, blood fanning out from the back of his head. The man is Farhan, a young jihadist shot dead by anti-terror police on a Solo street two weeks before our visit.

Farhan was an alumnus of the Ngruki school and the pictures and two separate stories describing his death were downloaded from radical Islamist websites, printed out and pinned up, presumably for their educational value. Depending on how it was spoken about, the story might have been placed there in mourning, or as an exhortation to righteous fury.

Asked about it, young English and Arabic teacher Abu Amar airily says the school teaches current events, just like any other. But this is not just any event. And there were no other posters on that board.

Abu Bakar Bashir's son Abdul Rohim is a senior teacher at the Ngruki school his father founded. He defends the teaching of jihad, saying: "More than 60 verses of the teaching of jihad are in the Koran. Should we delete those verses?"

## The Charge of a Conspiracy

Not all the verses are about violence or war. Some are about the struggle to be a good Muslim; others about the desirability of an Islamic state. But alumni such as Idris recall a focus, particularly in extracurricular activities, on the warlike verses.

## The Continuing Threat of Extremist Violence

The threat of extremist violence in Indonesia is not over, even though the last two years have seen major successes in breaking up extremist networks. One by one, men on the police most-wanted list have been tracked down, arrested, tried and imprisoned. The police have been good, but they have also been lucky. The would-be terrorists have been poorly trained, poorly disciplined and careless. The last major attack in Jakarta was in 2009, and the total number of people killed by terrorists in 2011 was five: three police and two of their own suicide bombers. A familiar sense of complacency has set in that the problem is largely over.

*International Crisis Group,*
*"How Indonesian Extremists Regroup,"*
*Asia Report, no. 228, July 16, 2012.*

Abdul Rohim bristles at any suggestion that this school is unusual, or its curriculum dangerous.

"Yes, some alumni of Ngruki are involved [in violence], but you cannot put the blame on the school," he says angrily. "It's so unfair. It's so irresponsible. It's a ridiculous way of thinking. For example, in your own country, if there's a thief or a rapist, would you put the blame on their school?"

The fact is that not just one, but many terrorists have been to Ngruki, including some of the linchpins of the Bali bombings. . . . In a recent series of terror raids in Indonesia, a number of the jihadis arrested or killed were also Ngruki alumni. Abdul Rohim says when such cases come to light, the current students are taught that "it's such a wrong action".

But his words are ambivalent at best. He refuses to call the Bali bombers terrorists, saying they were, at worst, misguided "mujahideen" (holy warriors). "Mujahid can make mistakes. What they did will not reduce their status as mujahideen. They must be judged by what is their intention," he says. "I don't want to even subtly claim that they were terrorists. It's a word used by non-Muslims to corner Islam."

Asked about the recent crop of alumni involved in terrorist activities, Abdul Rohim, like his father, claims a conspiracy. They were turned to terrorism by the police to discredit Islam, he says, even though a police officer was killed in one of their attacks. "Well, it's a conspiracy. Sometimes they are willing to sacrifice their own friends for the conspiracy. . . . It's a pretty normal thing for an intelligence officer to kill his own friends to cover up their own activities."

Abdul Rohim boasts that the school has been continuously accredited by the Ministry of Religious Affairs and the Ministry of Education [and Culture] for more than a decade. He says demand for places grew fast in the wake of the Bali bombing, and the school is still expanding. Posters around the campus show plans for new dormitories in new locations.

## An Anti-Terror Plan

Once radicals graduate from school or [leave] prison, the next stage is to be invited to join a training camp, or a plot. After the recent spate of arrests, there was a push for the government to establish a de-radicalisation program. Vice President Boediono himself ordered an anti-terror plan to be in place by next year, and said that the fight against radical ideas had been too sporadic. "This de-radicalisation blueprint will be comprehensive and will really serve the purpose," Boediono said.

But Irfan Idris, the head of the de-radicalisation program at the National Counterterrorism Agency, says the entire agency has a budget of only $9.5 million, of which only a part is set aside for the "soft approach" of de-radicalisation (as distinct from hard law enforcement).

An existing program running in Indonesian prisons since 2010 applies three strategies, he says: culture (using traditional Wayang puppet shows); business (trying to establish an economic base for prisoners); and ideology (countering the radical brainwashing). But in the past two years, only 32 prisoners nationwide have completed the program and there has been no attempt to measure its success.

*Once radicals graduate from school or [leave] prison, the next stage is to be invited to join a training camp, or a plot.*

Professor Sarlito Wirawan [Sarwono], a psychologist working on this program and others, says it can take up to three years to convince someone not to act on their radical theology. At this rate it would take decades to even talk to one year's supply of recruits from the radical boarding schools and the prisons. Asked about the radical boarding school in Ngruki, Irfan refers me to the Religious Affairs Ministry, which keeps accrediting the school.

## Programs in the Private Sector

There are also several private sector de-radicalisation programs. Noor Ismail Huda, a journalist and former student at Ngruki, says Indonesian authorities "have been doing extremely well after the milk has been spilled".

He runs a program of "disengagement", which involves having former radicals run cafes. Here they are forced to serve customers of all cultures and religions, and they can also make money, making his program self-sustaining. "We fight terrorism with doughnuts and coffee," he says.

So far, though, he has only three cafes, and has helped perhaps a handful of radicals.

Another private program is the Afghan Alumni Forum, where former radicals, the hard core who trained in Afghanistan, try to use their kudos in the jihadi community to put people on the right path.

It is led by Abu Wildan, a former senior teacher at Ngruki who was asked to join the Bali plot but refused. Abdul Rahman Ayub, Jemaah Islamiah's former deputy in Australia, is also a key member, as is one-time Bali plotter Maskur Abdul Kadir. It holds forums in suburban function rooms under a banner that reads: "Indonesia, peace without violence, terrorism and radicalism in the name of religion".

---

*Australia has proscribed organisations and passed laws against hate speech. People have been jailed for preaching terror. Indonesia has nothing similar.*

---

Psychologist Sarlito works with the forum and claims an 80 per cent success rate. He says attacking the ideology head-on simply did not work because the radical imams still hold such sway. "I'm not replacing anything. I leave their beliefs, but I say don't do this and this . . . don't start hurting people," he said.

"Then we bring in the wives, families, and say, 'How about helping each other?'. . . It's step by step and it takes three years. It's not an easy job."

As these well-meaning efforts continue, though, schools and prisons keep churning out radicals. Australia has proscribed organisations and passed laws against hate speech. People have been jailed for preaching terror. Indonesia has nothing similar.

And, according to Nasir Abbas, the highest-profile reformed member of Jemaah Islamiah, it will not develop them. "In Indonesia it's different. They let you build whatever ideology you want, set up a school, as long as you don't do the crime. . . . This is what people here call Reformasi," he says.

"We've got freedom of speech and expression. You can't just shut down a school."

# In the Western World, Racist Skinheads Are a Growing Danger

## Intelligence Project of the Southern Poverty Law Center

*In the following viewpoint, the Intelligence Project of the Southern Poverty Law Center argues that radical racist skinheads are a problem all over the world in countries with a white majority, with notable growth in the United States, Western Europe, and Russia. The author claims that although the skinhead movement did not start out as racist, it currently is a worldwide phenomenon that is radical, racist, and often violent. The Intelligence Project of the Southern Poverty Law Center is dedicated to monitoring hate groups and extremist activity in the United States.*

As you read, consider the following questions:

1. According to the author, when and where did the first skinheads emerge?
2. Which group, according to the author, was formed in 1994 in an attempt to unite the racist skinhead movement?
3. According to the author, what country currently has the worst skinhead problem in the world?

The racist skinhead movement in the United States has entered its fourth decade. Since the first skinhead gangs surfaced in Texas and the Midwest in the early 1980s, this racist and violent subculture has established itself in dozens of states from coast to coast and has authored some of the country's most vicious hate crimes in memory, from arson to assault to murder. The racist skinheads' trademark style—shaved head, combat boots, bomber jacket, neo-Nazi and white power tattoos—has become a fixture in American culture.

## A Global Movement

The scowling skinhead has joined the hooded Klansman [referring to the Ku Klux Klan] as an immediately recognizable icon of hate.

Unlike the Klan, racist skinhead culture is not native to the United States. And unlike the Klan, it is a truly global phenomenon, with skinhead gangs haunting major cities and towns in just about every white-majority country on earth. From Austria to Australia and Argentina to America, working-class youths can be found dressed in some local variation on the skinhead theme, espousing a crude worldview that is viciously anti-foreigner, anti-black, anti-gay, and anti-Semitic. In recent years, the Internet and cheap international airfares have allowed skinhead groups across the planet to communicate and organize in ways that would have shocked the original skinheads of the 1960s and '70s, whose vision and turf were limited to the East London neighborhoods in which they grew up and lived.

The growth of the racist skinhead movement has mirrored the rise in nonwhite immigration to the West. As the skin hues of Europe and North America have darkened with steady post–World War II immigration from Africa, Asia, and the Middle East, a nativist backlash has appeared in both mainstream and extremist forms. The skinhead movement is the most violent and ideologically crude form of this backlash.

Depending on the country, racist skinheads may have shadowy ties to radical parties participating in electoral politics. Skinhead groups in the U.S. lack such connections, but for those unlucky enough to encounter them on a darkened street, this does not make them any less fearsome.

## The Origins of the Skinhead Movement

The first skinheads emerged in the late 1960s as just one of the many distinct youth cultures that flowered in postwar [Great] Britain. Taking elements of English "mod" and Jamaican immigrant fashion, these working-class London youths crafted an identity in self-conscious opposition to the middle-class "long-hairs." At various points in their early development, English skinheads positioned themselves as tough working-class counterpoints to foppish mods, long-haired hippies, mohawked punks and made-up goths.

*It is a truly global phenomenon, with skinhead gangs haunting major cities and towns in just about every white-majority country on earth.*

The skinhead style first emerged as part of a non-racist and multiracial scene. White skinheads took on a persona that reflected admiration for and kinship with a new generation of working-class West Indian immigrants into the United Kingdom [UK]. Like the Jamaican immigrants of the time, the first skinheads were clean-cut, neat, and sharp-looking compared to the shaggier youth styles of the period. (White skinheads eventually lost their affinity for Jamaica as Rastafarian fashions became ascendant, with their overtones of black pride and pan-Africanism.)

Many early white skinheads were vaguely nationalistic and "proud to be British," but their deepest loyalties lay with their childhood chums and the local soccer team, not the "white race," as professed by today's racist skinheads. While known for their youthful aggression, petty criminality, and soccer stadium violence, this activity was seen as born out of economic hardship and a general spirit of bully-boy rebellion—not blind race hatred. Indeed, the first skinhead music was reggae and ska, both black musical forms; the earliest targets of white skinheads' anger and homemade weapons were each other and rival soccer fans.

## A Split in the Movement

But a split between racist and non-racist skinheads was apparent and began deepening soon after the style was born. By the early '70s, skinhead attacks on South Asian immigrants in London—the infamous sport of "Paki bashing"—had become an international news story. These violent skinheads had not yet acquired the trappings of neo-Nazi costumes and ideology, but they were already acting like [Adolf] Hitler's goon squads, the Brownshirts. One skinhead explained a typical "Paki bash" to a *Time* magazine journalist in 1970: "You go up to them and bump into them, and then you nut [forehead bash] them right, and then you hit them, and as they go down you give them a kicking, bash them with an iron bar, and take their watches and rings and things like that."

More than 50 such attacks were reported within a span of weeks in 1970, triggering street protests by British South Asians. A definitive break between racist and non-racist skins had occurred.

During the early to mid '70s, England's skinheads went into temporary decline. They experienced a revival in 1976, when a new generation of skinheads started earning a fresh reputation for violence through attacks on punks, homosexuals, and immigrants.

Fueling these attacks and cementing the new racist skinhead identity was increasing association with two neofascist political parties, the National Front and the British Movement. The latter, founded by longtime neo-Nazi Colin Jordan in 1968, did the most to stamp a swastika on the racist sector of the skinhead movement. The British Movement ran candidates in the 1974 U.K. general elections who espoused neo-Nazi ideas and wore swastikas while handing out party literature featuring the image and words of Adolf Hitler. In 1975, the British Movement gained a charismatic leader in the form of Michael McLaughlin, who reached out to the racist skinheads and appealed to their sensibilities and skills by emphasizing violence and street-level hate.

---

*A split between racist and non-racist skinheads was apparent and began deepening soon after the style was born.*

---

Between the arrival of Michael McLaughlin in 1975 and the election of Margaret Thatcher as British prime minister in 1979, the first hard-core neo-Nazi skinheads were born.

## The Skinhead Movement in the United States

The neo-Nazi skinhead phenomenon spread quickly to the United States. By the early 1980s, skinhead activity was reported in Texas and the Midwest, among other places. But the movement only started gaining national attention during the last third of the decade. It was then that skinhead gangs like the Dallas Hammerskins made a splash with violent racist attacks on immigrants and blacks.

The most important skinhead gang in raising the American movement's early profile was Chicago's CASH (Chicago Area Skinheads), which made national headlines with a brutal 1987 crime spree that involved assaults on six Hispanic women, swastikas painted on three synagogues, and numerous incidents of vandalism to Jewish-owned business. The leader of CASH was an ex-con and former member of the American Nazi Party named Clark Martell.

In the mid-1980s, Martell played the role of a skinhead Johnny Appleseed, performing around Chicago with his punk band Romantic Violence and passing out American Nazi Party newsletters and copies of *National Socialist* magazine between his band's sets. Martell's neo-Nazi recruiting drive caught the attention of Chicago's numerous "traditional," or non-racist, skinheads, including a number of African Americans. (According to Chicago punk lore, the city's skinhead scene was founded by black, non-racist skins.) Enjoying the advantage of vastly superior numbers, anti-racist crews such as Skinheads of Chicago (SHOC) routinely ganged up on CASH skins at shows and in the streets. "They grew out of what we are—the punk scene—so it's up to us to combat them," a member of the Chicago Anti-Racist Action (ARA) skinhead crew told the *Chicago Tribune*.

By the time Martell and the other five CASH skins were arrested for a gruesome 1987 attack on a former member, CASH had been more or less beaten into submission by anti-racist skins. But Martell had merely proven he was ahead of his time, and his defeat was local. When he first started re-cruiting for CASH, there were likely fewer than 200 racist skinheads in the United Sates. By 1989, when he was con-victed of home invasion, aggravated battery, and robbery and sentenced to 11 years in prison, there were an estimated 3,000.

## A Growth in the Movement

A major force behind this national growth spurt was Tom Metzger, a Fallbrook, Calif.-based former Klansman and long-time leader of the neo-Nazi group White Aryan Resistance (WAR). Around 1986, Metzger formed WAR Youth and launched an organized skinhead outreach campaign. Together with his teenage son, John, Metzger sought to ground the dis-persed movement in ideology and direct its wild and chaotic youthful energy into building smart, well-trained, and obedient street cells around the country. In 1988, Tom Metzger organized the first major hate-rock festival in the U.S., Aryan Fest, in Oklahoma.

It was also in 1988 that Metzger's efforts bore their most bitter fruit. In November, WAR youth representative Dave Mazzella visited Portland, Ore., to train and guide members of a local skinhead crew, East Side White Pride. During this visit, a group of Portland skins under Mazzella's tutelage attacked a group of Ethiopian immigrants in the middle of a street with steel-toed boots and a baseball bat. One of them, graduate student Mulugeta Seraw, died from his wounds. Although Metzger would later lose a bruising $12.5 million lawsuit brought against his organization by the Southern Poverty Law Center and the Anti-Defamation League—a suit that effectively wrecked WAR as an organization capable of putting skinheads into the street—he continues propaganda efforts to this day from a new base in Indiana. But Metzger's current operation is limited to a radio show and a website (resist.com) that is largely devoted to racist and anti-Semitic "humor."

The murder of Mulugeta Seraw was hardly unique during the American skinhead movement's growth years. Indeed, there were scores of brutal skinhead assaults around the country during the late '80s and early '90s, including the cold-blooded murders of black men in Birmingham, Ala., and Arlington, Texas.

Those responsible for these murders included members of the dreaded Confederate Hammerskins, a confederation of skinheads founded in Dallas in 1987. After spreading throughout the South, Hammerskin-affiliated gangs began appearing on the East and West Coasts in the early 1990s.

## An Attempt to Unite the Movement

It was out of these geographically disparate Hammerskin gangs that Hammerskin Nation (HSN) was formed in 1994. The idea was to unite all of the regional Hammerskin groups into

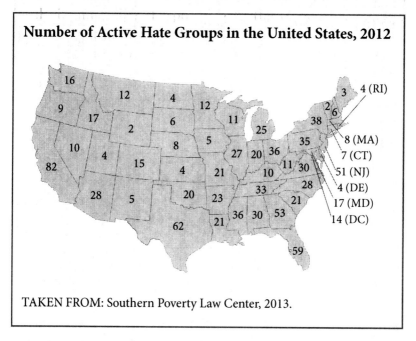

**Number of Active Hate Groups in the United States, 2012**

TAKEN FROM: Southern Poverty Law Center, 2013.

a national and even international force, with affiliated chapters in Europe. And for a while, the plan worked. Hammerskin Nation established itself as the most powerful skinhead organization in the country during the mid and late '90s. At its peak, HSN directed nearly 30 chapters and ran a successful record label, publishing house, and website. The HSN symbol of two crossed hammers swept the skinhead scene. And an annual meeting and concert, Hammerfest, was launched in 1999, allowing HSN members from around the world to meet and organize. Throughout this period of Hammerskin ascendancy, the racist skinhead movement continued to grow and was responsible for hundreds of racially motivated crimes around the country. It was also during this period, in 1997, that Denver police officer Bruce Vander Jagt became the first American police officer killed in the line of duty by a racist skinhead.

Hammerskin dominance failed to outlast the decade, however. As early as 1999, Hammerskins around the country were complaining in private and on message boards about the heavy-handed and "elitist" leadership style of the organization's top officers. The number of HSN chapters dropped off, with new regional groups rising up and loudly asserting their independence. Chief among these renegade skinhead groups were, first, the Outlaw Hammerskins, and then the Hoosier State Skinheads in Indiana and the Ohio State Skinheads, which in 2004 merged to form the Vinlanders Social Club, aka the Vinlanders. In 2005, the Vinlanders hosted the first Blood & Honour USA Council, a unity meeting of regional skinhead crews also known as the Council 28 (because B is the second letter of the alphabet and H the eighth), in Ohio. It is at this annual gathering that skins would, according to the Vinlanders website, "meet yearly with other crews and exchange ideas and debate direction and tactics." And drink lakes of beer, of course.

---

*There were scores of brutal skinhead assaults around the country during the late '80s and early '90s.*

---

Incredibly violent, full of swagger, and loathe to take orders from anyone, the Vinlanders were thought to represent the future in a more decentralized skinhead scene. But in the first weeks of 2007, Vinlanders founder Brien James, a particularly violent racist, posted a notice on the group's website announcing that the group was separating itself "from the racist movement." The announcement explained: "We do not see anything positive being accomplished, for our nation or our people, by participating in the white racialist movement as it stands. We have attempted to change this movement from within and have not succeeded. It is our opinion that a large number of the people involved in the greater movement are paid informants, social outcasts, and general losers in life."

But the fourth decade of skinheads in America finds skinhead groups growing. The number of skinhead groups has increased dramatically in recent years, totaling 133 by 2012.

These new groups are defined by a violent gangster ethos that is only partly informed by racist and neo-Nazi ideology.

## The Importance of Music

Along with exposure to extremist political parties and hate literature, music has always been a key element in the growth of the racist skinhead subculture. This is appropriate, as the original skinhead scene was based around clubs playing ska and reggae. The hard-driving rock and roll favored by today's racist skinheads both exploits and channels the youthful energy of members and potential teenage recruits.

---

*Along with exposure to extremist political parties and hate literature, music has always been a key element in the growth of the racist skinhead subculture.*

---

The importance of music in building the racist skinhead scene was apparent by the late '70s, when a hate-rock scene exploded alongside the punk rock movement, spreading lyrics that were anti-immigrant, anti-black, and anti-Semitic. Groups such as Skrewdriver, Skullhead, and No Remorse forged a common skinhead culture in sweaty, beer-soaked, makeshift concert halls, with lyrics professing brotherhood among whites and violent, uncompromising antagonism to outsiders of all kinds. The early hate-rock skinhead scene in Britain coalesced around what were known as the "Rock Against Communism" (RAC) concerts, the first of which was held in Leeds in 1978. RAC shows were organized in opposition to the earlier "Rock Against Racism" concerts, a series of musical events meant to counter growing racist currents in English culture. A subgenre of punk that often veered toward racism was known as Oi!, which soon became global (if not completely accurate) shorthand for skinhead music.

By the mid-1980s, a racist skinhead culture defined by loud hate-rock, cases of cheap beer, bloody "boot parties" directed against immigrants and others, and the flagrant display of neo-Nazi iconography and paraphernalia had spread to Western Europe and North America. Although focused on a skinhead gang in Melbourne, Australia, the 1992 Russell Crowe film *Romper Stomper* paints a particularly vivid and well-researched picture of the day-to-day life of skinheads immersed in this culture. (A later film that explored the racist skinhead culture, this one set in California, was 1998's *American History X*, starring Edward Norton.)

The importance of music in growing the worldwide skinhead movement cannot be overstated. William Pierce, leader of the neo-Nazi National Alliance until his death in 2002, understood well the potential impact of hate-rock. "Music speaks to us at a deeper level than books or political rhetoric: music speaks directly to the soul," said Pierce, author of the seminal hate-lit novel *The Turner Diaries*.

---

*The impact of U.S. hate-rock is not limited to the United States.*

---

## The Impact of Resistance Records

Putting this insight into practice, Pierce purchased the ailing hate-rock label and distributor Resistance Records in 1999 and built the company into a major force in the world skinhead movement. Resistance Records had been originally founded in 1993 by George Burdi, a young Canadian skinhead who also started the band RAHOWA (an acronym for Racial Holy War), which was one of the most popular and influential hate-rock bands of the period. Bernie Farber of the Canadian Jewish Congress has described Burdi as one of the most effective recruiters for the movement in history. (Burdi has since renounced hate and embraced Eastern mysticism.)

The first label to seriously challenge the dominance of Resistance Records was Minnesota-based Panzerfaust, named after a Nazi-era German anti-tank weapon. Before imploding amid a scandal involving the non-Aryan heritage of its founder, Anthony Pierpont, Panzerfaust was best known for a failed 2005 plan to distribute 100,000 hate-rock sampler CDs in school yards across the nation.

The impact of U.S. hate-rock is not limited to the United States. Since the production, performance, and distribution of such music is illegal in many countries in Western Europe, the U.S., with its First Amendment guarantees of free speech, has become a main provider of music to skinheads internationally (just as U.S. computer servers host most European hate sites in order to keep their owners clear of European anti-hate legislation). This relationship was built in part by the outreach programs of Resistance Records under George Burdi, who used to offer Eastern Europeans CDs at 90% discounts, as well as free license to reproduce the music.

New media platforms—including social networking sites like MySpace and Twitter and video file-sharing sites like You-Tube—are being used by racist skinhead groups to recruit and expose others to their views.

## The International Scene

The connections between racist skinheads in the U.S. and Europe are not limited to hate-rock catalogs. With the rise of the Internet, groups scattered across the globe have been able to communicate and link up as never before, transforming the skinhead movement from an exclusively neighborhood-based phenomenon into a global culture with common points of reference and even annual events. The ease with which interested parties can access hate literature and music online has also given rise to the phenomenon of the "Internet Nazi"—young fellow travelers who are not part of organized skinhead gangs but who profess allegiance to the movement's code and support purveyors of skinhead paraphernalia with online orders.

The country with the worst skinhead problem today is Russia, where it is estimated there are tens of thousands of active neo-Nazi skinheads, including thousands in the capital alone. In recent years, immigrants, students and even senior embassy staff from Asian and African nations have been the victims of assaults and murders on the streets of Moscow.

---

*Across Europe, radical parties are on the rise, exploiting fears over immigration.*

---

As in Western European countries, Russian skinhead violence often dovetails with soccer hooliganism. A 2002 report in the *Nation* described the trend:

"In the past few years a curious synthesis of the soccer hooligan and skinhead movements has been observed steadily gaining strength in the city. It's no longer uncommon in Moscow to see crowds of 300–400 soccer fans—dressed in the black bomber jackets and black boots popularized by German skinheads—loitering on the streets in the city's outer regions, and not always on the same nights as soccer matches."

Some of these skinheads, the article notes, have been seen wearing the armbands of the neo-Nazi Russian National Unity party, suggesting links between street hate and organized political parties. Such links are suspected to be common in many Western European countries, where radical parties participate in electoral politics in recent years with sobering success.

Across Europe, radical parties are on the rise, exploiting fears over immigration. In several of these countries, associations have been traced between skinhead gangs and parties with representatives in regional and national bodies.

# In Germany, Right-Wing Extremism Is on the Rise

**Spiegel Online**

*In the following viewpoint,* Spiegel Online *reports that a recent nationwide survey found that from 2010 to 2012, there was an increase in right-wing extremist views in Germany, particularly in former East Germany and in rural areas.* Spiegel Online *reports that researchers have found that advanced education is correlated with less extremism, categorizing education as protective against such attitudes.* Spiegel Online *is the online English international edition of Germany's print weekly* Der Spiegel.

As you read, consider the following questions:

1. According to the author, what percentage of Germans hold xenophobic attitudes?

2. Between 2010 and 2012, how much did the prevalence of right-wing attitudes rise in states of former East Germany, according to the viewpoint?

3. According to the author, the erosion of solidarity can be seen in the marginalization of what three groups?

As Germany continues to grapple with the fallout of the discovery of the murderous far-right terrorist group the National Socialist Underground (NSU), researchers have come to the "unsettling" conclusion that right-wing extremist thought has increased in the country.

*Spiegel Online,* "Not Just on the Fringes: Far-Right Attitudes Increase in Germany," November 12, 2012. Reproduced by permission.

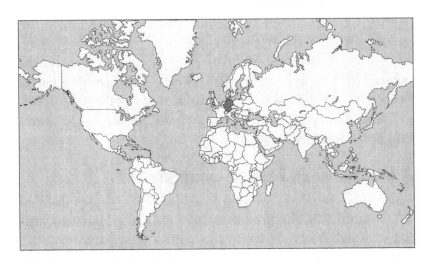

## An Increase in Right-Wing Extremism

Just last week [November 8, 2012], federal prosecutors formally charged the last surviving member of the neo-Nazi NSU, which is suspected of committing 10 murders, two bomb attacks and 15 armed robberies in the last 12 years. The case shocked Germany when it broke last year, bringing the issue of right-wing extremism to the forefront of public debate. Though some argue that it exists only on the fringes of society, the researchers behind the study released on Monday conclude that these attitudes are widespread throughout Germany.

Starting in 2006, the Friedrich Ebert Foundation [also known as Friedrich-Ebert-Stiftung], which has ties to the center-left Social Democratic Party (SPD), began publishing "Movement in the Middle," a series of biannual nationwide surveys the organization calls a "barometer of current anti-democratic attitudes in Germany."

Since the publication of the last results in 2010, the foundation has registered an increase of right-wing extremist attitudes from 8.2 to 9 percent across the country, with xenophobia found to be the most prevalent manifestation, a prejudice held by 25.1 percent of the population. The development demands attention, the researchers say.

"Action at all levels—whether it is in education work, the media, civil society or democratic parties—is urgently needed," the report says. "Because the approval that right-wing extremist messages receive within the German population is unsettling for a number of reasons."

## A Sharp Rise in Eastern Germany

The study, based on surveys conducted in the summer of 2012, found that the prevalence of right-wing extremist attitudes varied greatly according to region. Compared to 2010, western German states actually showed a slight reduction, down from 7.6 percent to 7.3 percent overall. But there was a strong jump in the states that belonged to the former East Germany, up from 10.5 to 15.8 percent, the highest level ever measured by the researchers, who say it continues to rise.

*The prevalence of right-wing extremist attitudes varied greatly according to region.*

According to their estimation, the region's weak economy is largely to blame. When it comes to anti-foreigner sentiment, the study found that some 20 percent of western Germans hold such attitudes, compared to 39 percent of people in the east. Since 2004, that figure has fallen from about 25 percent in the west, but risen from one-quarter of all people in the east.

Unlike the results of previous surveys, this time young people from eastern Germany aged 14 to 30 showed a higher level of approval for things like a right-wing authoritarian dictatorship, chauvinism, social Darwinism and the trivialization of National Socialism [Nazism], than those over the age of 60. And while on a national average every eleventh German has anti-Semitic attitudes, levels were higher in eastern Germany than in the west for the first time.

"It is especially worrying that the study shows a new generation of right-wing extremism," the authors write. While in the past young people were considered to be less susceptible to these ideas, now it is exactly this group that stands out. "The structural problems in eastern Germany, which have still not been adequately addressed even 20 years after reunification, are reflected here, as is this generation's feeling that they are not needed," they add.

Still, the researchers warned against classifying the problem as an eastern German one, explaining that socioeconomic structures have far more influence than location. Big cities like Hamburg and Berlin, for example, showed more heartening results than rural areas. People from urban areas with more immigrants, it turns out, exhibited greater tolerance.

For the first time, the study included respondents who did not have German citizenship, finding that these people often feel politically and socially marginalized. It is "not surprising," the study says, that immigrants showed lower levels of right-wing extremist attitudes.

## Education Is a Key Factor

"The basis for right-wing extremist attitudes in Germany remains high," the study's authors conclude. While they were optimistic in 2010 that strengthened social structures would be enough to combat such a development, this time their conclusion is "more cautious," they add.

---

*Education is the leading "protective factor" against the further spread of right-wing extremist thought.*

---

Another factor behind the trend seems to be a measurable "erosion of solidarity" within society, which results in the marginalization of not just immigrants, but also those struggling to get by in society like the unemployed and homeless.

# The Potential for Conflict in Germany

There is growing potential for social, religious, and ethnic conflict in Germany. On the one hand, the country harbors militant right-wing extremists who do not shy away from violence and murder. On the other hand, German society at large has become more cosmopolitan, diverse, and individualistic. Fewer and fewer people, particularly those who dwell in major metropolitan areas, do not have at least some foreign or immigrant ties in their families or circles of friends. In 2011, the steadily growing percentage of people with an immigrant background stood at 19.5%, or about one-fifth of the population. . . . Enormous and far-reaching attitudinal differences exist, both between residents of cities and residents of rural areas and between young and old people, concerning respect for diversity (in a broader sense that includes, but is not exhausted by, ethnic diversity). For example, there tends to be less tolerance for independent choice of personal identities or preferences in rural areas.

In fact, at least with respect to the general population, the acceptance of plurality and individualism has increased noticeably during the past few decades. Nevertheless, certain specific dimensions of misanthropic thinking, such as anti-Semitism, xenophobia, chauvinism, and Islamophobia, are quite widespread and have actually grown among some segments of the population recently.

*Britta Schellenberg,*
*"Right-Wing Extremism and Terrorism in Germany:*
*Developments and Enabling Structures,"*
*in* Right-Wing Extremism in Europe: Country Analyses,
Counter-Strategies and Labor-Market Oriented
Exit Strategies. *Eds. Ralf Melzer and Sebastian Serafin.*
*Berlin: Friedrich-Ebert-Stiftung, 2013.*

Education is the leading "protective factor" against the further spread of right-wing extremist thought, though. According to the study, people who complete university-track secondary education programs are far less likely to hold such views than those who do not. More civic and educational programs are needed to combat this issue, the study concludes, and it also calls on the media to remember its responsibility to release balanced reports on these issues.

# The Paranoid—and Growing—Militia Threat

## Marilyn Mayo

*In the following viewpoint, Marilyn Mayo argues that there has been a disturbing rise in far-right extremism groups in the United States. Mayo claims that these antigovernment groups have the potential for violence, and many recent events illustrate the groups' violent tendencies. She contends that there is a real danger that the groups could get a stronger foothold in the mainstream, leading to increased violence. Mayo is codirector of the Anti-Defamation League's Center on Extremism.*

As you read, consider the following questions:

1. According to the author, on what antigovernment group has the press tended to focus?

2. Between 2008 and 2010, the militia movement in the United States grew by the addition of how many groups, according to Mayo?

3. According to the author, what is the name of the militia group that targets current and former law enforcement and military personnel for recruitment?

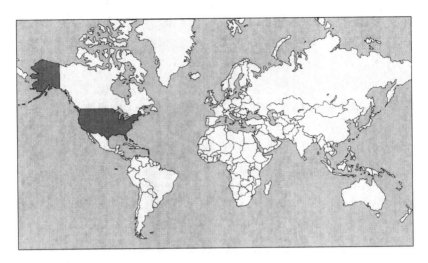

Over the last year and a half, far-right extremism has blossomed, fueled by an intense distrust and hatred of the federal government in general and of President [Barack] Obama in particular. To antigovernment extremists, including a growing number of militia groups, the government is not only dangerous but an actual enemy to be defeated.

Pennsylvania hasn't been immune to this rise in antigovernment extremism, particularly the increase in militia activity. In January [2010], a number of small militia groups planned to conduct paramilitary training in the Michaux State Forest. Another schedules similar monthly training in an unnamed location.

Both the economic crisis and the election of a president seen by many as "foreign" are contributing to this antigovernment sentiment, which has also found its way into the mainstream.

The press has focused on the comparatively mainstream tea-party movement as the antigovernment cause du jour. But it's the extremist groups that vilify the government the most and have the greatest potential for violence.

In March, members of the Hutaree militia in Michigan and elsewhere were charged with allegedly plotting to kill law enforcement officers and possibly their families. Their aim was to spark an armed confrontation with the government that they thought would lead to an uprising.

Disturbingly, though, the Hutaree is just one of scores of new militia groups that have sprung up in the last two years. Between 2008 and 2010, the militia movement has grown from about 50 groups nationally to nearly 200. Many groups are preparing for what they believe is an inevitable confrontation with federal authorities. Their beliefs are driven by conspiracy theories that paint the government as a tyranny poised to imprison or kill "dissidents."

---

*It's the extremist groups that vilify the government the most and have the greatest potential for violence.*

---

In many cases, antigovernment sentiment can give way to threats. In April, Walter Fitzpatrick, an antigovernment extremist, tried to arrest officials in Tennessee after a grand jury refused to consider a complaint he attempted to file claiming that President Obama was an illegal alien and should be arrested for treason. After authorities arrested Fitzpatrick on various charges, another antigovernment extremist and militia member, Daniel Huff, traveled from Georgia to allegedly arrest those officials and free Fitzpatrick.

Although Huff, too, was stopped by police, there are other conspiracy-driven antigovernment groups that have shown a willingness to take violent action. In May, Jerry Kane and his teenage son were driving through eastern Arkansas when West Memphis police pulled them over during a drug-interdiction operation. The Kanes came out of the car with weapons and killed the two officers before speeding away. They were killed in a second shootout with police, during which they injured two more officers.

The Kanes were members of the extreme antigovernment "sovereign-citizen" movement, which has also exploded in growth over recent years. It's a loose collection of groups and individuals who believe that virtually all government in the U.S. is illegitimate, having been subverted by an evil conspiracy. They seek to restore their vision of the original government through a variety of means, including violence.

The notion of the government as enemy has spread to increasingly wider circles. "The greatest threat we face today is not terrorists," wrote a retired Arizona sheriff, Richard Mack, on his Web site. "It is our own federal government. If America is conquered or ruined it will be from within, not a foreign enemy."

Mack is a prominent member of the Oath Keepers, a group formed in 2008 that targets current and former law enforcement and military personnel for recruitment. The Oath Keepers claim they'll refuse to carry out certain "orders" that they expect the federal government to issue, such as putting citizens in concentration camps, assisting foreign troops in invading the country and declaring martial law.

These fantasies reflect the degree to which the Oath Keepers consider the government a sinister enemy. And their ranks are growing—Mack was able to attract over a thousand people to a recent speaking engagement in Idaho, and he is in high demand.

When people can convince themselves that the government is the enemy, they can also talk themselves into taking action, including violent measures like those allegedly taken by the Hutaree and the Kanes. And there's a danger that extremism can gain a foothold in the mainstream, subverting or replacing legitimate criticism of the government. If that happens, the violence we have seen so far will only grow.

# Periodical and Internet Sources Bibliography

*The following articles have been selected to supplement the diverse views presented in this chapter.*

| | |
|---|---|
| Anti-Defamation League | "Post-9/11 Islamic Extremism in the U.S.," 2012. |
| Michael Bachelard | "Terrorist Cell May Still Be Active," *Sydney Morning Herald* (Australia), October 7, 2012. |
| Ben Doherty | "Where Extremism Rules," *Sydney Morning Herald* (Australia), April 8, 2011. |
| Mohamed Eljarh | "Pushing Back Against Libya's Extremists," *Foreign Policy*, May 17, 2013. |
| Afyare Abdi Elmi | "Somalia: A Time for Caution," Al Jazeera, July 14, 2010. |
| Abraham H. Foxman | "The Resurgence of the Militia Movement," *Huffington Post*, April 15, 2010. |
| Azeem Ibrahim | "What Does 'Moderate' Mean in Malaysia?," *Huffington Post*, October 12, 2012. |
| Juliane von Mittelstaedt | "Advance of the Zealots: The Growing Influence of the Ultra-Orthodox in Israel," *Spiegel Online*, January 13, 2012. |
| David Newman | "Israel Must Stamp Out Jewish Extremism," *Jerusalem Post*, October 10, 2011. |
| Steven Plaut | "Israel's Tenured Extremists," *Middle East Quarterly*, Fall 2011. |
| Andrew Rosenkranz | "Extremist Groups Find Home in Florida," *South Florida Sun-Sentinel*, July 31, 2011. |
| Haroon Siddiqui | "Extremism Elsewhere, Moderation in Canada," *Toronto Star*, April 25, 2012. |

GLOBALVIEWPOINTS

CHAPTER 2

# The Causes of Extremism

# In Africa, State Weakness Leads to a Rise in Extremist Groups

*Zachary Devlin-Foltz*

*In the following viewpoint, Zachary Devlin-Foltz argues that Africa's fragile states create an environment that allows Islamic extremists to gain public acceptance and political power. Devlin-Foltz contends that in failed states without adequate security such as Somalia, Islamic extremists fill the void of political power and Islamic moderates tend to adopt violence. He claims that although state security operations can neutralize extremists in the short term, as in Egypt and Algeria, this is an insufficient long-term strategy. Devlin-Foltz is an independent researcher.*

As you read, consider the following questions:

1. Devlin-Foltz claims that how many of the twelve "high-risk" states in Africa have populations that are one-third or more Muslim?

2. According to the author, what is the main moderate Islamist organization in Egypt, and what is the main extremist Islamist organization?

Zachary Devlin-Foltz, "Africa's Fragile States: Empowering Extremists, Exporting Terrorism," *Africa Security Brief*, no. 6, Africa Center for Strategic Studies, August 2010. Copyright © 2010 by Africa Center for Strategic Studies. All rights reserved. Reproduced by permission.

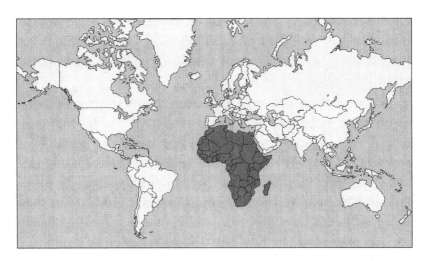

3. Since what year has Somalia essentially been without a government, according to Devlin-Foltz?

Twelve of the twenty states deemed by the Failed States Index (FSI) to be at greatest risk of collapse in 2010 are in Africa. These fragile and failed states account for much of the continent's ongoing conflict, instability, and humanitarian catastrophes. State failure raises the risk of personal insecurity, lawlessness, and armed conflict. Such persistent and randomized insecurity undermines all aspects of ordinary life, forcing people to stay in their homes and close their businesses for fear of violence. Under such circumstances, residents become willing to support or accept virtually any groups that are able to restore order—be they warlords, local gangs, or organized criminal syndicates.

## Islamic Extremists in Africa

Among the violent actors that fill the power vacuums of Africa's fragile and failed states are Islamist extremists. By providing security and basic services, they hope to gain greater public acceptance of their ideological agendas. A state's failure to assert a monopoly on legitimate force accordingly opens the door for extremists to build their bases of political power.

Of the twelve "high-risk" states in Africa, eight have populations that are one-third or more Muslim, a feature that more than doubles a state's risk of instability and provides fertile ground for Islamist extremists.

Many of these countries have seen the increasing influence of Islamists in recent years. Islamists share the belief that politics, as well as personal life, should be based on Islam. They envision an ideal Islamic state in which shariah, Islamic law, forms the basis for political authority. Most Muslims in Africa are not Islamists. And most Islamists are not violent. But their rising influence coincides with recent threats posed by violent African extremists. In July 2010, Somalia's Islamist militia al-Shabaab detonated three simultaneous explosions that targeted two venues in Kampala, Uganda, showing the final World Cup match, killing nearly 80 Ugandans and foreigners. Islamic militancy has also been growing across the Sahel, fueling concerns that this will spawn more terrorism in Africa. African Islamists, furthermore, have been implicated in terror plots on the continent and abroad. Perhaps the most high-profile case concerned Umar Farouk Abdulmutallab, a Nigerian who attended Islamist schools in Yemen and allegedly attempted to set off a bomb on a U.S.-bound airliner on December 25, 2009.

*Among the violent actors that fill the power vacuums of Africa's fragile and failed states are Islamist extremists.*

The platform certain Islamist movements provide extremist ideologies can also create an incubator for international terrorists, much as the rise of the National Islamic Front in Sudan and the Taliban in Afghanistan in the 1990s led to the sheltering of al Qaeda. If not properly engaged, then, Africa's active Islamist movements pose a serious danger to security at the individual, national, and international level. However, common misperceptions of Islamist movements have led to misguided policies to curb their influence. A better understanding of Islamists and how their relationship with broader society changes in the context of state fragility can inform more effective counter-extremism and counterterrorism policies in Africa.

## Fragile States and Islamist Movements

Though their adherents often share broad long-term goals, moderate and extremist Islamists do not work together in most stable states. Both may seek a shariah government, but extremists' use of violence strikes most moderates as counterproductive, costly, and wrong. Conversely, extremists judge moderates to be in dereliction of their religious duties for their refusal to adopt jihad, or holy war.

This changes when a state is weak or fails. If a government does not credibly provide security and a peaceful means for moderates to pursue their political ends, moderates may come to see violence as their best or only option. If moderates remain nonviolent under such conditions, they risk loss of credibility, not to mention attacks and intimidation from groups that do use force. But if moderate Islamists' use of violence helps to reestablish local stability, they can gain support even from those who do not share their ideology. Once moderates take this step, however, whether out of political strategy or necessity, the main barrier to their cooperating with extremists disappears. The effect is to empower extremists, who gain greater credibility and acceptance from larger swaths of the population.

In short, there is a general inverse relationship between extremist Islamists' influence and state strength. In stable contexts, extremists tend to occupy a marginal fringe of the political space. As the level of fragility increases, however, they tend to move to center stage. The state, moderates, extremists, and other actors accordingly adapt their goals and strategies to changing circumstances. This fragility-extremism nexus has unfolded in a variety of ways in Africa.

## Islamic Organizations in Egypt

The Muslim Brotherhood (MB) is Egypt's most well-known moderate Islamist organization. Its extremist counterpart, Egyptian Islamic Jihad (EIJ), has waged violent jihad for over 30 years and is a key component of al Qaeda. Both groups believe that Muslim societies should be governed by Islamic shariah states. However, the Muslim Brotherhood has remained essentially peaceful for the last few decades, pursuing its agenda through social programs and electoral competition. By contrast, Egyptian Islamic Jihad has employed violence consistently throughout its existence. The MB and EIJ criticize each other bitterly. The Brothers call the jihadis' terrorism dangerous and counterproductive while the extremists denounce the MB for luring young Muslims away from holy war.

---

*There is a general inverse relationship between extremist Islamists' influence and state strength.*

---

EIJ's founding leaders began their Islamist careers in the Brotherhood. They broke away in the late 1970s following over a decade of brutal state oppression in which hundreds of Brothers were arrested and many executed. The crackdowns convinced many of these young Islamists that the Egyptian regime was waging a war on Islam and that Muslims had a duty to resist violently, however high the costs. By contrast, the MB's moderate leaders concluded that violence would only invite more oppression while alienating an Egyptian public that preferred peace.

Egypt's capable security sector exploited this wedge between moderates and extremists to further weaken the EIJ. It launched another round of violent oppression, this time specifically targeting extremists for imprisonment and torture.

Such repression raised the costs of Islamist violence such that only those who saw holy war as a duty, or at least a glorious pursuit, remained committed to it. Though it officially remains banned, the Brotherhood became Egypt's primary opposition party, and many experts believe it would win a truly free and fair election today [in 2010]. Meanwhile, as the extremists were isolated and were languishing in jails or in hiding, their political clout waned. Intermittent domestic terrorist campaigns during the 1990s kept EIJ and other extremists in the headlines but never translated into political power. By the late 1990s, most extremists had renounced violence, whereas the remaining EIJ hard core ultimately moved abroad and joined al Qaeda's international jihad.

## Islamist Organizations in Algeria

Algeria provides a similar example in which the state used a combination of oppression and amnesty to push moderate Islamists away from violence. However, just as in Egypt, that policy unintentionally drove Algeria's most extreme Islamists to join al Qaeda, forming al Qaeda in the Islamic Maghreb (AQIM) in 2006. During a bloody civil war that raged for most of the 1990s, brutal violence won Islamist rebels little more than heavy-handed repression from the state and political alienation from the public. Many Algerians originally sympathized and supported the Islamists after the military nullified the 1991 elections they were likely to lose. However, as the civil war raged on and the violence grew more shocking and seemingly gratuitous, the public and most Islamists grew tired of the destruction. Violence, for them, was a means to an end, and they abandoned it once it proved ineffective. By the mid-2000s, only the extreme Salafist Group for Preaching and Combat, known by its French acronym GSPC, remained armed and active.

Just as had happened in Egypt, Algerian extremists who refused to renounce violence alienated the general populace

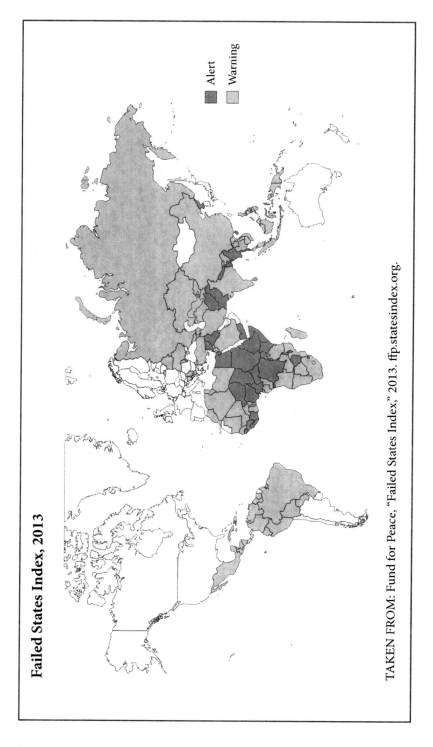

Failed States Index, 2013

Alert

Warning

TAKEN FROM: Fund for Peace, "Failed States Index," 2013. ffp.statesindex.org.

and a mainstream Islamist movement that preferred peace. Whereas the GSPC's extremist predecessor recruited up to 500 new fighters a week during the 1990s, recent estimates of the GSPC's and AQIM's manpower rarely exceed 1,000. Stripped of its moderate members and politically marginalized, the group joined al Qaeda hoping to find abroad the relevance it lost at home.

Algeria's and Egypt's robust security measures were able to target extreme Islamists and dissuade moderates from pursuing strategies of violence. However, while extremist violence proved a costly and unproductive strategy in Egypt and Algeria, moderates have been provided few opportunities for nonviolent political participation. This perpetuates the ongoing tension among Islamists over the respective benefits of peaceful engagement versus violence. Moreover, while the extremist threat is subdued, it persists. . . .

## The Islamist Split in Somalia

Since its 1991 civil war, Somalia essentially has been without a government. Left stateless for so long, Somalis have created various local institutions designed to fill in for official government in essential areas. Starting in the mid-1990s, neighborhood leaders established shariah courts to provide law and order. Originally, most courts focused on securing the streets, limiting their activities both geographically and politically to reflect the priorities of ordinary residents and clan and business leaders.

By 2005, however, more ambitious Islamists had managed to organize many courts into a loose coalition called the Union of Islamic Courts (UIC). The UIC's leadership included both moderates, concerned mostly with security and maintaining public support, and extremists bent on coercing their way to an Islamic state. They joined together to fight Somalia's many predatory warlords. For moderates, defeating the warlords consolidated the UIC's power and pleased their constituents.

For extremists, the warlords, some of whom received U.S. support to pursue al Qaeda suspects, were agents of the West and the chief obstacle to jihad in Somalia. Protracted state collapse and its attendant chaos unified these enemies and temporarily superseded their many differences.

*While extremist violence proved a costly and unproductive strategy in Egypt and Algeria, moderates have been provided few opportunities for nonviolent political participation.*

The UIC never achieved full unity of command, and its more moderate leaders struggled to control their extremist allies. Nevertheless, the coalition might have held for some time had Ethiopia not invaded Somalia in December 2006 to remove what it saw as a threat on its border. The incursion split the Islamists. The extremists, most notably the group al-Shabaab, launched an underground insurgent campaign, while many moderate UIC leaders decided to negotiate with the Ethiopians. In effect, the presence of Ethiopian troops made violence less productive for the moderates, who could no longer build support by taking and securing territory.

For the extremists, however, the Ethiopian invasion brought a foreign, non-Muslim army into the equation—and against which they could rally nationalist and Islamist sentiments. Al-Shabaab went on to declare itself an al Qaeda affiliate. Though al Qaeda operatives had long used Somalia as a place to hide and stage attacks elsewhere, al-Shabaab provided the organization its first significant foothold in local Somali politics.

The Islamist split in Somalia continues. Even after Ethiopian troops withdrew in 2009 and the moderate Islamist Sharif Sheikh Ahmed became president of a government of national unity, al-Shabaab remained in the armed opposition, preferring to fight the moderates rather than join them in peace.

For their part, most non-Islamist power brokers, be they clan elders or businesspeople, continue to prioritize security and their own local authority. Some strike deals with al-Shabaab, some with other armed groups, and still others with the government. Though each no doubt has ideological preferences, the overriding necessity of securing self, family, and business drives them to side with whoever can most credibly protect or threaten them. . . .

## The Fragility-Extremism Nexus

Islamism is a complicated ideology, and its interaction with national politics and the state only adds to the complexity. Nevertheless, as experiences in Egypt, Algeria, Nigeria, Somalia, Mali, and Senegal demonstrate, certain patterns emerge. States with capable security sectors, such as Egypt and Algeria, make violence a costly strategy, driving a wedge between moderates and extremists by prompting the former to renounce violence. By contrast, in states that are unable to provide adequate security, moderates may adopt violent strategies to capitalize on the public's desire for stability and to defend themselves from those who take up arms. Indeed, where no overarching authority can punish those using violence for political means, all politics is likely to become violent. This enables extremists to find common cause with moderates without any change in either group's underlying ideologies.

Such political gains make extremists much more influential in failed states than in stable ones. That influence allows them to frustrate subsequent stabilization efforts. Somalia's al-Shabaab is a prime example of this phenomenon. Having exploited the state's weakness to form coalitions with moderate Islamists and gain backing, or at least acquiescence, from non-Islamist leaders, the group continues to forcefully resist efforts to rebuild the Somali state, in part because al-Shabaab recognizes that its influence would decline dramatically in a stable society. In contrast, while Nigeria is in many ways a deficient state, it has sufficiently capable institutions to make violence a costly strategy for extremists. Armed resistance would provoke a powerful government response and cost moderates the influence they enjoy within the current system.

---

*Where no overarching authority can punish those using violence for political means, all politics is likely to become violent.*

---

But state strength alone provides only a temporary fix to the threat of extremists. The Egyptian and Algerian states maintain their control with heavy-handed methods and have accumulated poor human rights records. Their brutal approach, however, further radicalizes extremists, pushing them toward al Qaeda. With their moderate members sheared off, prospects for domestic political gains slim, and their own passions hardened by conflict, imprisonment, and torture, extremists have more reason than ever to join the global jihad.

# Muslim Blowback? Muslims in the United States Are Relatively Well Integrated into Society. So, Why the Recent Spate of Attacks Carried Out by US Muslims?

*M. Junaid Levesque-Alam*

*In the following viewpoint, M. Junaid Levesque-Alam argues that the recent increase in terrorist attacks and plots in the United States by Muslim Americans illustrates that Muslims in America are not as well assimilated as is often believed. Levesque-Alam contends that US military intervention abroad has not only fueled hatred of America in Muslim countries, but also has led to the domestic radicalization of some Muslim Americans who undertake domestic terrorist activities. Levesque-Alam is a regular contributor to* Foreign Policy in Focus; *he has published in Altmuslim.com,* CounterPunch, WireTap Magazine, *and* ZNet; *and his website is Crossing the Crescent.*

As you read, consider the following questions:

1. The author cites a poll finding what percentage of Muslim Americans describe themselves as "thriving"?

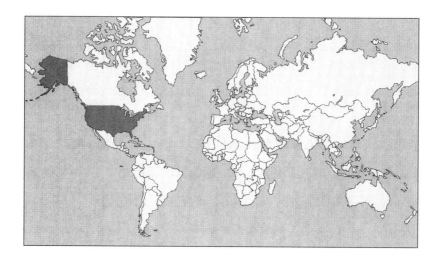

2. According to Levesque-Alam, what fraction of homicides committed in the United States in 2009 were attributable to Muslim militancy?

3. What quote by President Barack Obama does the author use in support of his claim that support is growing for the view that military interventionism increases extremism?

It is hard to overstate just how deeply unpopular the United States is in the Muslim world.

A 2008 poll of six majority Muslim countries found that overwhelmingly large portions of the population, ranging from 71 percent in Morocco to 87 percent in Egypt, held unfavorable opinions of the United States. A 2009 poll in Pakistan revealed that 64 percent of the public views the United States as an outright enemy.

So it is a curious paradox that, despite the antagonistic and sometimes violent relationship between the United States and the Muslim world, Muslims here have fared relatively well. According to a 2009 Gallup poll, 41 percent of Muslims in the United States describe themselves as "thriving"—only five percentage points below the national average, and higher than the percentage reported in any Muslim country aside from Saudi Arabia. A full 40 percent say they have at least a college degree, making them the second-most educated religious group after Jews (at 61 percent).

Further, U.S. Muslim women, after their Jewish counterparts, are the most highly educated female religious group in the country, and Muslim economic gender parity is the nation's most egalitarian at both the low and high ends of the spectrum.

An earlier 2007 Pew study painted a similar picture. Titled *Muslim Americans: Middle Class and Mostly Mainstream*, it described the Muslim minority in the United States as "largely assimilated, happy with their lives, and moderate with respect to many of the issues that have divided Muslims and Westerners around the world."

Events of the last few months, however, have called into question the pertinence, if not the validity, of that rosy general assessment. Though terrorist suspects had in the past almost always been foreigners, several of those implicated in more recent plots against American soldiers and civilians were Muslims born or raised in the United States.

## U.S. Muslims as a Domestic Threat

The November 2009 incident at Fort Hood, the Texas army base where Maj. Nidal Hasan is suspected of gunning down 10 fellow soldiers, presents the most striking case. A steady stream of unsuccessful plots has also garnered attention: the 25-year-old Queens coffee vendor who pleaded guilty to a conspiracy to destroy the New York City subway system in September 2009; the five youths who left Washington, D.C., in December 2009 allegedly to join a Pakistani militant group; the middle-aged, self-proclaimed convert from Philadelphia who reportedly planned to kill a Swedish cartoonist last month; the 25-year-old New Jersey man who was caught in Yemen a week later purportedly trying to join al-Qaeda.

And just this Monday, one day after the most recent terror scare, police arrested a 30-year-old naturalized U.S. citizen from Pakistan; they suspect him of having loaded a sport-utility vehicle with the bomb-making materials that were designed to explode in the most iconic part of our country's most celebrated metropolis: Times Square, New York City.

---

*Several of those implicated in more recent plots against American soldiers and civilians were Muslims born or raised in the United States.*

---

Although attention lavished on individual cases should not obscure the broader picture—of the 14,000 homicides committed in the United States last year, only 14 are attributable to Muslim militancy—the sudden swell of homegrown Muslim extremism is significant. Most acutely, it has thrust into the foreground questions that have lingered in the minds of many Americans since September 11: Does Islam cause terrorism? Are all Muslims potential terrorists?

For conservatives, the latest string of incidents will only harden their conviction that the answer is a resolute "yes." They have long insisted that Islamist terror isn't fueled by policy or circumstance but is instead an article of the Islamic faith. And where no trace of terror can be found, conservatives have gleefully cooked up charges against Muslims, as illustrated by the smear campaigns directed at Swiss academic Tariq Ramadan, former Obama adviser Mazen Asbahi, Organisation of the Islamic Conference envoy Rashad Hussain, and the original principal of New York City's first Arabic-language school, Debbie Almontaser.

For some liberals, too, the recent developments will cause unease. It was one thing to face attacks from abroad, but the presence of a homegrown Muslim threat seems to shatter the old shibboleths about multiculturalism and diversity. Some on the left had neatly apportioned Muslims into categories of

The Causes of Extremism

"good" and "bad," and the old paradigm that accepted only "assimilated" and "modernized" Muslims as safe is now under threat.

This liberal unease has already reached an advanced stage in Britain, typified by the writer Martin Amis, who insists that he despises "Islamism" but not Islam. This qualification notwithstanding, Amis regularly lets his mask slip with puffed-up declamations such as this one: "[N]o doubt the impulse toward rational inquiry is by now very weak in the rank and file of the Muslim male."

In fact, there is a shared element between conservative and liberal views on Islamist extremism: certainty that the main problem lies with Muslims themselves.

---

*The notion that our violence motivates terrorism has always lost out to the notion that terror is absent from our violence.*

---

## Their Violence, Our Violence

The palatable and politically safe answers—for conservatives, that Muslims are inherently violent, and for left-liberals, that only a small minority is violent—have always skirted around one important detail: our own violence.

This is no surprise. The notion that our violence motivates terrorism has always lost out to the notion that terror is absent from our violence. It was George Orwell who observed in 1945 that "the nationalist not only does not disapprove of atrocities committed by his own side, but he has a remarkable capacity for not even hearing about them."

But this "remarkable capacity" is not shared by everyone. Civilian deaths and accounts of torture from Iraq, Afghanistan, and Palestine have fueled the radicalization of a minority of Muslims abroad, and it was only a matter of time before it produced the same effect on a minority of Muslims here, too.

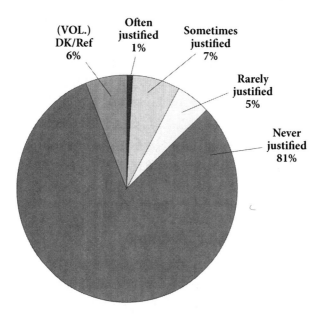

**Muslim American Opinion on Violence**

*Some people think that suicide bombing and other forms of violence against civilian targets are justified in order to defend Islam from its enemies. Other people believe that, no matter what the reason, this kind of violence is never justified. Do you personally feel that this kind of violence is often justified to defend Islam, sometimes justified, rarely justified, or never justified?*

TAKEN FROM: Pew Research Center Survey, April 14–July 22, 2011.

It is only now, amid this growing domestic radicalization, that we are seeing some willingness to cure the deafness Orwell once wrote about.

## Hope for the Future?

In a December 2009 *New York Times* article, top U.S. terrorism experts spoke bluntly about what motivates these attacks. Bruce Hoffman, a terrorism researcher at Georgetown University, noted that American military interventionism was the only logical reason for the spike in homegrown terror cases. "The longer we've been in Iraq and Afghanistan, the more some susceptible young men are coming to believe that it's their duty to take up arms to defend their fellow Muslims," he said. Robert Leiken, from the Nixon Center in Washington, D.C., echoed that theme: "Just the length of U.S. involvement in these countries is provoking more Muslim Americans to react."

---

*That some Muslim extremists now hail from our own country has, paradoxically, brought us closer to curbing terrorism.*

---

In March, the Center for Strategic and International Studies went a step farther. In its 22-page report on homegrown terrorism, it not only recognized the motives of homegrown terrorist suspects but advised the government to shift its policy accordingly:

> [S]everal of those arrested last fall seemed to harbor the belief that the United States is at war with Islam. . . . The United States must continue to work to puncture this narrative. White House officials already have discarded phrases like 'war on radical Islam.' But ultimately, the United States needs to go further than this, because al Qaeda seizes on more than just U.S. rhetoric to galvanize support for its agenda; the group also points to America's military presence in Muslim countries as evidence for its preferred narrative. The United States, then, should consider how to balance the need to combat global terrorism with the drawbacks of large-scale, direct military intervention.

That study, along with a January report co-issued by Duke University and the University of North Carolina, also urged the government to open more lines of communication with the Muslim community.

The Obama administration at least appears to be listening on both counts.

In an April 14 speech, the president broke with a long tradition of enforced silence by asserting that the Israeli-Palestinian crisis has ended up "costing us significantly in terms of both blood and treasure." Ignoring the cacophony of neoconservative complaints, the administration has also allowed Tariq Ramadan back into the United States and defended its choice of Rashad Hussain as special envoy to the Organisation of the Islamic Conference.

Moreover, Arab and Muslim community leaders feel they are finally being heard. "For the first time in eight years, we have the opportunity to meet, engage, discuss, disagree, but have an impact on policy," said James Zogby, president of the Arab American Institute in Washington. "We're being made to feel a part of that process and that there is somebody listening."

These moves are encouraging. That some Muslim extremists now hail from our own country has, paradoxically, brought us closer to curbing terrorism. It is doubtless more difficult to conjure fantastic and absurd explanations for suicide attacks—endless virgins, inexplicable evil, exotic culture—when those carrying out such attacks are integrated and functioning members of our society rather than easily caricatured foreigners.

If the Obama administration follows through on its hesitant first steps, scaling down its military interventions, tempering its support for Israeli colonialism, and increasing engagement efforts with Muslims here and elsewhere, it will lay down a solid framework for building trust and respect.

As Audrey Kurth Cronin of the National War College observed, those assets are valuable in combating militancy: "To me, the most interesting thing about the five [Virginians] is that it was their parents that went immediately to the F.B.I. It was members of the American Muslim community that put a stop to whatever those men may have been planning."

For ten years, America has hitched its foreign policy train to an engine of war and occupation. As a result, America's standing in the Muslim world has declined disastrously. It's long past time to switch tracks.

# In Norway, Islamophobia Is Causing Right-Wing Extremism

## Aslak Sira Myhre

*In the following viewpoint, Aslak Sira Myhre argues that a recent terrorist attack in Norway shows that one of the causes of right-wing extremism is Islamophobia. Myhre argues that the immediate assumption that the attack was by Islamic extremists, coupled with the media treatment of the issue once the true terrorist was identified, illustrates that further attention is needed toward growing intolerance in Europe. Myhre is the director of the House of Literature in Norway, an author, and the former leader of the Red Electoral Alliance.*

As you read, consider the following questions:

1. The author argues that political violence in Norway in recent decades has been perpetrated almost exclusively by what groups?
2. What reason does Myhre suggest that Norwegians immediately looked for al Qaeda after the terrorist attack?
3. Myhre claims that the madness of the Norwegian terrorist has what two distinct kinds of causes?

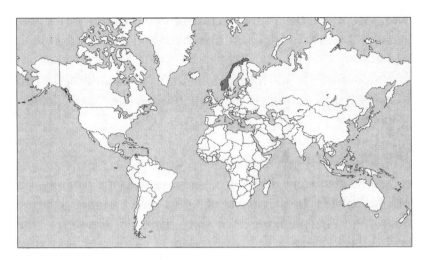

Like every other citizen of Oslo, I have walked in the streets and buildings that have been blown away. I have even spent time on the island where young political activists were massacred. I share the fear and pain of my country. But the question is always why, and this violence was not blind.

## Political Violence in Norway

The terror of Norway has not come from Islamic extremists. Nor has it come from the far left, even though both these groups have been accused time after time of being the inner threat to our "way of living". Up to and including the terrifying hours in the afternoon of 22 July [2011], the little terror my country has experienced has come from the far right.

For decades, political violence in this country has been almost the sole preserve of neo-Nazis and other racist groups. During the 1970s they bombed left-wing bookstores and a May Day demonstration. In the 80s two neo-Nazis were executed because they were suspected of betraying the group. In the past two decades, two non-white Norwegian boys have died as a result of racist attacks. No foreign group has killed or hurt people on Norwegian territory since the Second World

War, except for the Israeli security force Mossad, which targeted and killed an innocent man by mistake on Lillehammer in 1973.

But even with this history, when this devastating terror hit us, we instantly suspected the Islamic world. It was the jihadis. It had to be.

## The Immediate Assumption

It was immediately denounced as an attack on Norway, on our way of life. In the streets of Oslo, young women wearing hijabs and Arab-looking men were harassed as soon as the news broke.

Small wonder. For at least 10 years we have been told that terror comes from the East. That an Arab is suspicious, that all Muslims are tainted. We regularly see people of colour being examined in private rooms in airport security; we have endless debates on the limits of "our" tolerance. As the Islamic world has become the Other, we have begun to think of that what differentiates "us" from "them" is the ability to slaughter civilians in cold blood.

*The terrorist was a white Nordic male; not a Muslim, but a Muslim hater.*

There is, of course, another reason why everybody looked for al-Qaida. Norway has been part of the war in Afghanistan for 10 years, we took part in the Iraq war for some time, and we are eager bombers of Tripoli [the capital of Libya]. There is a limit to how long you can partake in war before war reaches you.

But although we all knew it, the war was rarely mentioned when the terrorist hit us. Our first response was rooted in irrationality: It had to be "them". I felt it myself. I feared that the war we took abroad had come to Norway. And what then? What would happen to our society? To tolerance, public de-

## Islamophobia in Europe

Prejudice towards Muslims is often greater than that experienced by other religious or ethnic minority groups. In the UK [United Kingdom] Baroness [Sayeeda Hussain] Warsi has commented that Islamophobia is seen as normal, and that prejudice against Muslims does not carry the same social stigma as prejudice towards other ethnic and religious groups. Islamophobia is promoted by both extremist political parties as well as mainstream parties to gain votes and popularity generally. In the Czech Republic for instance, extremist parties are mainly responsible for any open intolerance towards Muslims in the political sphere. While in France, Islamophobia is used across the political spectrum; the left casts Islam as a threat to the sacred principle of 'laïcité' [secularism] whilst the right presents Islam as a threat to the French way of life. In Finland, reference is made to 'immigration-critical' politicians of the True Finns Party and the fact that members of the party, including a member of European Parliament (MEP), have been fined by the court for expressing anti-Muslim views on blogs.

*European Network Against Racism, "Racism in Europe: ENAR Shadow Report 2011–2012," March 2013, p. 13.*

bate, and most of all, to our settled immigrants and their Norwegian-born children?

It was not thus. Once again, the heart of darkness lies buried deep within ourselves. The terrorist was a white Nordic male; not a Muslim, but a Muslim hater.

## The Role of Islamophobia and Racism

As soon as this was established, the slaughter was discussed as the deed of a mad man; it was no longer seen as primarily an attack on our society. The rhetoric changed, the headlines of the newspapers shifted their focus. Nobody talks about war anymore. When "terrorist" is used, it is most certainly singular, not plural—a particular individual rather than an undefined group which is easily generalised to include sympathisers and anyone else you fancy. The terrible act is now officially a national tragedy. The question is, would it have been thus if the killer was a mad man with an Islamic background?

I also believe that the killer was mad. To hunt down and execute teenagers on an island for an hour, you surely must have taken leave of your senses. But just as 9/11 [referring to the September 11, 2001, terrorist attacks on the United States] or the bombing of the subway in London, this is madness with both a clinical and a political cause.

Anyone who has glanced at the web pages of racist groups or followed the online debates of Norwegian newspapers will have seen the rage with which Islamophobia is being spread; the poisonous hatred with which anonymous writers sting anti-racist liberals and the left is only too visible. The 22 July terrorist has participated in many such debates. He has been an active member of one of the biggest Norwegian political parties, the populist right party until 2006. He left them and sought his ideology instead among the community of anti-Islamist groups on the Internet.

---

*We need to use this incident to strike a blow to the intolerance, racism and hatred that is growing, not just in Norway, nor even only in Scandinavia, but throughout Europe.*

---

When the world believed this to be an act of international Islamist terrorism, state leaders, from [US president Barack] Obama to [prime minister of the United Kingdom David] Cameron, all stated that they would stand by Norway in our struggle. Which struggle will that be now? All Western leaders have the same problem within their own borders. Will they now wage war on homegrown right-wing extremism? On Islamophobia and racism?

Some hours after the bomb blast, the Norwegian prime minister, Jens Stoltenberg, said that our answer to the attack should be more democracy and more openness. Compared to [former US president George W.] Bush's response to the attacks of 9/11 there is good reason to be proud of this. But in the aftermath of the most dreadful experience in Norway since the Second World War I would like to go further. We need to use this incident to strike a blow to the intolerance, racism and hatred that is growing, not just in Norway, nor even only in Scandinavia, but throughout Europe.

# Foreign Military Intervention in Afghanistan and Pakistan Is Fueling Extremism

*Sikander Shah*

*In the following viewpoint, Sikander Shah argues that the military operations conducted in Afghanistan and Pakistan have set a dangerous precedent and threaten international peace and security. Shah contends that US drone attacks in Pakistan are without proper legal justification and are fueling extremism. He concludes that the role of powerful states should be to focus on diplomacy and dialogue, rather than military operations. Shah is a legal fellow at the Institute for Social Policy and Understanding.*

As you read, consider the following questions:

1. According to the author, what justification did the United States give for military action in Afghanistan?

2. What is a large part of the reason, according to Shah, that civilian casualties far outnumber those of combatants in Pakistan?

3. In what manner does the author propose that the international community has a role to play in halting the current strategies in Afghanistan and Pakistan?

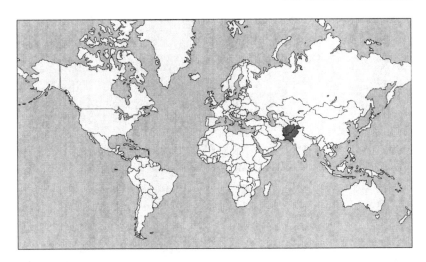

The tragic "friendly fire" incident at the weekend [November 26, 2011], in which 24 Pakistani soldiers were allegedly killed in a NATO [North Atlantic Treaty Organization] air strike, raises many questions. Who shot first? How should Pakistan respond? What is the future for the already traumatized U.S.-Pakistan relationship?

But surely the biggest question, after a decade of conflict, is this: Should the United States even have launched military action in Afghanistan in the first place? And was the magnitude of the attacks on September 11, 2001, so great as to mean there was no choice but to launch military operations?

## A Dangerous Precedent

Setting aside the support of the international community, the United States still chose to act unilaterally against Afghanistan, claiming self-defense. There was much debate at the time over the legality of the initial use of force. Yet the devastation that the people of Afghanistan and Pakistan have experienced over the last decade as U.S. and coalition forces have battled Taliban militias almost makes that debate seem trite.

Interestingly, the justification for the war has transformed from self-defense, to an even less well-defined fight against global terrorism. Meanwhile, Pakistan-based Taliban have replaced al-Qaeda as the central enemy in a war that has gradually come to be seen by Afghans as regime enforcement.

Whatever the reason given for military action, it has become increasingly clear that a dangerous precedent was set in Afghanistan. The justification for the use of force as self-defense has been increasingly utilized by opportunistic states to meet the challenge of insurgents and rebels, and this unwanted development of the doctrine of preemptive and preventive self-defense now poses a grave threat to international peace and security.

---

*The justification for the war has transformed from self-defense, to an even less well-defined fight against global terrorism.*

---

In addition, it also appears to be a mistake for coalition forces, acting under the mandate of the UN [United Nations] Security Council, to indulge in peace enforcement rather than just peacekeeping initiatives in Afghanistan. After all, history has shown that such aggressive use of force has typically worsened conflicts, as witnessed in Somalia.

## The Use of Drone Attacks

Indeed, as underscored by events at the weekend, the fight against Taliban militants has now spilled over into Pakistan, where civilian casualties far outnumber those of combatants. This is in large part due to the U.S. insistence of using drone attacks to target militants, attacks that have had only sporadic success, even as they have killed scores of civilians, thus fueling extremism and resentment in Pakistan.

Against this backdrop, the United States has avoided providing proper legal justification for drone attacks, which violate Pakistani sovereignty. When confronted on the issue, the [President Barack] Obama administration responds in vague terms that it has a right to defend itself. The Pakistani military, for its part, has generally stayed quiet over the issue.

Yet although the U.S. and Pakistani governments may have until recently been in tacit agreement over the drone strikes, these extrajudicial killings should be seen as illegal under international law, in violation of the Constitution of Pakistan, and without the support of the people of Pakistan.

This isn't to dismiss the dangers posed by Taliban militants, which are very real. The fostering of an environment of repression and intolerance—the Talibanization of society in the Pakistan-Afghan border regions—has created a level of anarchy that challenges the very fabric of society. It must be halted before irreparable harm results. But tackling Talibanization requires a multifaceted approach that as well as recognizing the reasons behind this process, also mandates addressing the root causes of radicalism and militarism. This approach should center on the peaceful resolution of all disputes, the fostering of nation-building through political dialogue and compromise, the strengthening of democracy, and the supremacy of the rule of law. Poverty, corruption and ethnic discrimination also need to be systematically addressed.

## The Role of Powerful States

How can the United States most usefully contribute? By immediately bringing to a halt its aggressive military strategy. Specifically, the U.S. should immediately stop drone attacks in both Afghanistan and Pakistan, withdraw its troops from Afghanistan at the earliest possible time and in the interim, U.S. and ISAF [International Security Assistance Force] forces should only partake in peacekeeping operations. Also, the U.S. and others shouldn't provide unaccounted for military aid to the Pakistan Army.

The Pakistani establishment, for its part, should look more to nonmilitary means of dealing with the conflict. For a start, it should engage in genuine political dialogue with militants in control of the FATA [Federally Administered Tribal Areas] regions to try to find a political solution to the conflict without compromising its position on sovereignty in relation to both the U.S and the militants. In addition, it should also institute measures to guarantee that its armed forces are conducting all operations in a transparent manner, in compliance with human rights and international humanitarian law. In this respect the media, civil society and humanitarian organizations must be allowed to function independently in war-torn areas.

---

*Unilateralist behavior by powerful states who achieve their objectives while violating the territorial sovereignty of weaker states is extremely damaging to interstate norms.*

---

And the international community also has a role to play, not least by being more proactive in trying to influence U.S. and NATO forces in the Pakistan-Afghan region. In addition, it should also hold Pakistan more accountable for its violation of human rights treaties and international law, and take concrete measures that respect local values, customs and religion, but which also improve protections for human rights. After all, aggression against civilians is not only a violation of the Geneva Conventions, but also the Islamic Law of Nations.

Ultimately, unilateralist behavior by powerful states who achieve their objectives while violating the territorial sovereignty of weaker states is extremely damaging to interstate norms. Instead, powerful nations should resist the temptation to flex their muscles and instead focus on diplomacy, political dialogue, and compromise—and the international community should put pressure on them to do so.

Such an approach isn't just right in and of itself, but will also give greater impetus to the development and recognition of multilateral judicial institutions that are best placed to address conflicts.

# Muslim Radicalization Stems from a Lack of Mainstream Islamic Education

*Azeem Ibrahim*

*In the following viewpoint, Azeem Ibrahim argues that Islamic education can prevent violence caused by radicalized Islamists. Ibrahim contends that most violent Islamists lack an education in mainstream Islamic teachings. He claims that in countries such as Egypt and Saudi Arabia, imprisoned radicals have been de-radicalized by giving voice to credible Muslim authorities who renounce violence. Ibrahim is the executive chairman of the Scotland Institute and a fellow at the Institute for Social Policy and Understanding.*

As you read, consider the following questions:

1. The author points to a study finding that radicalization of Muslims occurs in what four distinct stages?
2. For what reason does Ibrahim claim that radical Islamists reject and undermine traditional Islamic authority?
3. What respected Islamist thinker wrote an influential book renouncing terrorism, according to the author?

Azeem Ibrahim, "Tackling Muslim Radicalization: Lessons from Scotland," Institute for Social Policy and Understanding, June 2010, pp. 2–4. Reproduced by permission.

The dangers posed by radicalization are clear. Less well publicized are the results of the numerous academic studies on how it occurs. Yet some good evidence is available. For example Marc Sageman, a former CIA [Central Intelligence Agency] operations officer, has conducted the largest survey of radical Muslims to date in order to locate the causes for radicalization. In a groundbreaking study, he analyzed over 500 profiles and concluded that this phenomenon normally occurs in four distinct stages:

1. It is sparked when the individual reacts with moral outrage to stories of Muslims suffering around the world;

2. for some, that spark is inflamed by an interpretation that explains such suffering in the context of consistent policies in Western countries that are viewed as hostile to Muslims around the world;

3. the ensuing resentment is fuelled by negative personal experiences in Western countries (e.g., discrimination, inequality, or just an inability to get on despite good qualifications); and

4. the individual joins a terrorist network that becomes like a second family, albeit one closed to the outside world. This situation stokes the radical worldview and prepares the initiate for action and, in some cases, martyrdom.

The crucial stage is reached when a young Muslim begins to believe that Islam justifies vigilante justice and closes his/her mind to other viewpoints. To prevent such a situation, this radical ideology must be cut off at the roots by challenging radical interpretations of Islam, such as those that explain Muslim suffering in terms of a Manichaean war between Islam and the West or teach that Islam condones violence against civilians. If this is to be done successfully, young Muslims must be engaged directly and be exposed to other viewpoints.

## The Lack of Islamic Education

The clearest sign that a formal mainstream Islamic education prevents violence is the tiny percentage of violent Islamists who have actually received it. Reza Aslan, a research associate at the University of Southern California's Center on Public Diplomacy in Santa Monica, argues that almost 90% of violent Islamists have had no religious education at all. For example, none of those who carried out the 9/11 [referring to the September 11, 2001, attacks on the United States] or the 7/7 [referring to the July 7, 2005, bombings in London] attacks had received such an education. Even al-Qaeda's leadership lacks religious credibility. . . . Most of its leaders have backgrounds in medicine, engineering, or business. Osama bin Laden has no formal religious training and never attended a seminary. He dropped out of a university in Jeddah, where he was studying economics and management. Ayman al-Zawahiri is a qualified medical doctor. Abu Musab al-Suri, [according to Aftab Ahmed Malik,] "one of Al Qaeda's leading military thinkers," studied mechanical engineering but did not complete his degree. Eventually, he established his own import-export business. Abd al-Qadir b. Abd al-Aziz [also known as Sayyid Imam al-Sharif], one of "the most influential Egyptian Islamist theorists," also lacks a formal religious education. Of the 9/11 hijackers, bin Laden declared that they did not belong to any traditional school of Islamic law. The point is clear: If radical Islamists were educated as Muslim scholars, they would have known that what they advocate contravenes Islamic ethics and norms. These radical Islamists do not subscribe to traditional Islam; rather, they reject and undermine traditional authority because it is the very force that would deny them their modus operandi.

In [Great] Britain, radicalization has been exacerbated by a lack of mainstream Islamic education for young Muslims. In some areas this gap has been filled by radical preachers, unqualified in Islamic law and theology and normally from outside of Europe, who have replaced traditional pietistic, Islam with an ignorant, "pamphlet-based" Islam that emphasizes politics. Quintan Wiktorowicz, author of *Radical Islam Rising: Muslim Extremism in the West*, notes that the most susceptible young people are those who are not in a position to objectively evaluate whether a credible understanding of Islam is being provided or not. Most of them are, in fact, religious novices exploring their faith in depth for the first time.

> *The clearest sign that a formal mainstream Islamic education prevents violence is the tiny percentage of violent Islamists who have actually received it.*

Thus, the best way to prevent radicalization and the terrorism it allows is simply to educate our young people in mainstream Islamic teachings so that they will be able to recognize and, after placing such radical narratives, dubious theology, or ignorant preaching in their proper contexts, reject them. For radical Islamists, mainstream Islamic scholarship and ethics are a very real—perhaps the largest—threat.

## A Strategy for Preventing Islamic Radicalization

The shootings at Fort Hood, the arrests of five young men in Pakistan, and last summer's arrests of terrorism suspects in North Carolina mark a troubling increase in terrorism-related activity by Muslim Americans.

A 2010 report, "Anti-Terror Lessons of Muslim American Communities," conducted by scholars at Duke University and the University of North Carolina at Chapel Hill, provides one of the most thorough analyses yet of the extent of Muslim American radicalization and terrorism. It finds that although the number of radicalized individuals remains small, keeping it that way requires a defined strategy.

Among its recommendations are that policy makers reinforce the anti-radicalization activities currently under way in such communities and emphasize community-building and internal self-policing. David Schanzer and fellow researchers came to these conclusions after analyzing interviews with more than 120 Muslim Americans, as well as websites and publications belonging to Muslim American organizations, data on prosecutions of Muslim Americans for terrorism-related offenses, and existing studies of Muslim American communities.

The tactic of undermining radicalization's intellectual conditions has already succeeded in those countries that have tried it properly. Egypt and Saudi Arabia, which have used these tactics for many years, have de-radicalized imprisoned radicals by drawing attention to credible Muslim (and sometimes ex-Islamist) authorities who have renounced violence.

---

*The tactic of undermining radicalization's intellectual conditions has already succeeded in those countries that have tried it properly.*

---

For example, Dr. Sayyid Imam al-Sharif [also known as Abd al-Qadir b. Abd al-Aziz] is a respected Islamist thinker whose works have influenced leading al-Qaeda figures. But in 2007 he published *Rationalizing Jihad in Egypt and the World*, in which he renounced terrorism in the strongest terms possible. In an interview with the Egyptian press, he argued that his book posed an acute problem for al-Qaeda because none of its members or leaders are qualified, from a Shari'ah perspective, to respond. Many Muslim governmental and religious figures, understanding al-Sharif's authority among the Islamists, understood the potential value of his personal de-radicalization story; not surprisingly, it quickly became front-page news in many Islamic countries. Many Muslim scholars sided with al-Sharif, and al-Qaeda was stung into writing a two-hundred-page response. Western governments could re-peat this success by drawing attention to authorities who are credible to potential radicals.

# Periodical and Internet Sources Bibliography

*The following articles have been selected to supplement the diverse views presented in this chapter.*

| | |
|---|---|
| Kamran Bokhari | "The Challenge of Combating Militancy," *Express Tribune* (Pakistan), June 10, 2013. |
| John Campbell | "A Better Way to Keep Islamists at Bay in Mali," *Christian Science Monitor*, February 5, 2013. |
| John Feffer | "All-American Bigotry," *Huffington Post*, January 6, 2012. |
| H.A. Hellyer | "A Murder in Woolwich," *Foreign Policy*, May 25, 2013. |
| Ed Husain | "Egypt Risks the Fire of Radicalism," *New York Times*, July 3, 2013. |
| Azeem Ibrahim | "Comment: Why We Need to Change Our Tactics," *Scotsman* (Edinburgh, Scotland), May 26, 2013. |
| Muqtedar Khan | "Egypt, Tunisia, and the Death of Osama bin Laden," *Huffington Post*, May 2, 2011. |
| Peter A. Olsson | "Homegrown Terrorists, Rebels in Search of a Cause," *Middle East Quarterly*, Summer 2013. |
| Fouad Pervez | "Down with Drone War Silence," Common Dreams, November 21, 2012. |
| David Schanzer | "It's Time to Confront the 'Counterjihadists,'" *Globe and Mail* (Toronto, Canada), July 28, 2011. |
| Rachel Woodlock | "Anti-Muslim Tub-Thumping Helps Extremists," *Sydney Morning Herald* (Australia), March 23, 2011. |

**GLOBAL**VIEWPOINTS

## CHAPTER 3

# Extremism and Religion

# In the United States, Muslims Are Unfairly Suspected of Extremism

## Matthew Harwood

*In the following viewpoint, Matthew Harwood argues that American law enforcement is focused on preventing violent terrorist activity by Muslim Americans, even though the data do not support the focus on this group instead of Christian right-wing extremists. Harwood also claims that within the justice system Muslim Americans get treated unfairly, citing the different treatment in court of members of a Christian militia extremist group and an Islamic extremist. Harwood is a writer and a media strategist at the American Civil Liberties Union in Washington, DC.*

As you read, consider the following questions:

1. The author says what terrorist attack failed to increase surveillance of conservative Christians?

2. The author cites a study by the National Consortium for the Study of Terrorism and Responses to Terrorism (START), finding how many homicides by right-wing terrorists between 1990 and 2010?

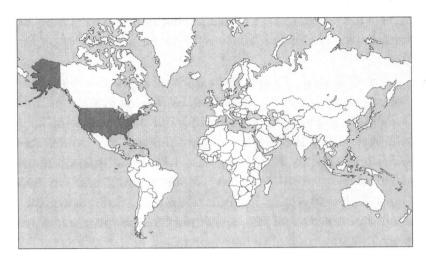

3. Harwood claims that both Tarek Mehanna and the members of Hutaree militia engaged in what constitutionally protected activity?

The evangelical Christians of Greenville County, South Carolina, are afraid.

There has been talk of informants and undercover agents luring young, conservative evangelicals across the South into sham terrorist plots. The feds and the area's police want to eliminate a particularly extreme strain of evangelical Christianity opposed to abortion, homosexuality, and secularism, whose adherents sometimes use violent imagery and speech. They fear such extreme talk could convince lone wolves or small groups of Christian extremists to target abortion clinics, gay bars, or shopping malls for attack. As a result, law enforcement has flooded these communities with informants meant to provide an early warning system for any signs of such "radicalization."

Converts, so important to the evangelical movement, are now looked upon with suspicion—the more fervent, the more suspicious. In local barbecue joints, diners, and watering holes, the proprietors are careful not to let FOX News linger on-screen too long, fearing political discussions that could be misconstrued. After all, you can never be too sure who's listening.

Come Sunday, the ministers who once railed against abortion, gay marriage, and Hollywood as sure signs that the U.S. is descending into godlessness will mute their messages. They will peer out at their congregations and fear that some faces aren't interested in the Gospel, or maybe are a little too interested in every word. The once vibrant political clubs at Bob Jones University have become lifeless as students whisper about informants and fear a few misplaced words could leave them in a government database or worse.

Naturally, none of this is actually happening to evangelical Christians in South Carolina, across the South, or anywhere else. It would never be tolerated. Yet the equivalents of everything cited above did happen in and around the New York metropolitan area—just not to white, conservative, Christian Americans. But replace them with American Muslims in the New York area and you have a perfect fit, as documented by the recent report "Mapping Muslims[: NYPD Spying and Its Impact on American Muslims]." And New York is hardly alone.

## The Surveillance of Muslim Americans

Since 9/11 [referring to the September 11, 2001, terrorist attacks on the United States], American law enforcement has taken a disproportionate interest in American Muslims across the country, seeing a whole community as a national security threat, particularly in California and New York City. But here's the thing: The facts that have been piling up ever since that date don't support such suspicion. Not at all.

The numbers couldn't be clearer: Right-wing extremists have committed far more acts of political violence since 1990 than American Muslims. That law enforcement across the country hasn't felt similarly compelled to infiltrate and watch over conservative Christian communities in the hopes of disrupting violent right-wing extremism confirms what American Muslims know in their bones: to be different is to be suspect.

In the aftermath of 9/11, law enforcement has infiltrated Muslim American communities and spied on them in ways that would have outraged Americans, had such tactics been used against Christian communities after the Oklahoma City bombing in 1995, or after any of the other hate crimes or antiabortion-based acts of violence committed since then by right-wing extremists.

Documents obtained through Freedom of Information Act requests by the American Civil Liberties Union make clear that FBI [Federal Bureau of Investigation] agents in California used community outreach programs to gather intelligence at mosques and other local events, recording the opinions and associations of people not suspected of any crime. In 2008, the FBI loosened its internal guidelines further, allowing agents to collect demographic information on ethnically concentrated communities and map them for intelligence and investigative purposes.

There is no question that the most extreme example of such blanket, suspicionless surveillance has been conducted by the New York City Police Department (NYPD). As revealed by the Associated Press, the NYPD's Intelligence Division carried out a secret surveillance program on the city's varied Muslim communities based on the erroneous belief that their religion makes them more susceptible to violent radicalization.

---

*The numbers couldn't be clearer: Right-wing extremists have committed far more acts of political violence since 1990 than American Muslims.*

---

## The New York Surveillance Program

The program, which continues today, looks something like this, according to "Mapping Muslims": "rakers," or undercover officers, are sent into neighborhoods to identify "hot spots"—mosques, schools, restaurants, cafes, halal meat shops, hookah bars—and told to chat up people to "gauge sentiment," while setting up "listening posts." "Crawlers," or informants, are then recruited and sent to infiltrate mosques and religious events. They are ordered to record what imams and congregants say and take note of who attended services and meetings.

These crawlers are encouraged to initiate "create and capture" conversations with their targets, bringing up terrorism or some other controversial topic, recording the response, and then sharing it with the NYPD. The intelligence unit also went mobile, checking out and infiltrating American Muslim student groups from Connecticut to New Jersey and even as far away as Pennsylvania.

When news of the NYPD's spying program broke, it shattered trust within the city's Muslim communities, giving rise to general suspicion and fraying community ties of all sorts. This naturally raises the question: How many terrorism plots were identified and disrupted thanks to this widespread and suspicionless surveillance program? The answer: none.

Worse, the chief of the NYPD Intelligence Division admitted in sworn testimony last summer that the Muslim surveillance program did not even generate a single criminal lead. The incredibly invasive, rights-eroding program was a complete bust, a total waste of the resources of the New York City Police Department.

And that's without even considering what is surely its most harmful aspect: the likelihood that, at least in the short term, it has caused irreparable damage to the Muslim community's trust in the police. Surveillance, concludes the "Mapping Muslims" report, "has stifled constitutionally protected activity and destroyed trust between American Muslim communities and the agencies charged with protecting them."

When people fear the police, tips dry up, potentially making the community less safe. This is important, especially given that the Muslim American community has helped prevent, depending on whose figures you use, from 21%–40% of all terrorism plots associated with Muslims since 9/11. That's grounds for cooperation, not alienation: a lesson that would have been learned by a police department with strong ties to and trust in the community.

*When news of the NYPD's spying program broke, it shattered trust within the city's Muslim communities.*

## The Number of Terrorist Attacks

The idea that American law enforcement's mass surveillance of Muslim communities is a necessary, if unfortunate, counterterrorism tool rests with the empirically false notion that American Muslims are more prone to political violence than other Americans.

This is simply not true.

According to the National Consortium for the Study of Terrorism and Responses to Terrorism (START), right-wing terrorists perpetrated 145 "ideologically motivated homicide incidents" between 1990 and 2010. In that same period, notes START, "al Qaeda affiliates, al Qaeda–inspired extremists, and secular Arab Nationalists committed 27 homicide incidents in the United States involving 16 perpetrators or groups of perpetrators."

Last November, West Point's Combating Terrorism Center published a report on America's violent far-right extremists. Its numbers were even more startling than START's. "The consolidated dataset," writes report author Arie Perliger, "includes information on 4,420 violent incidents that occurred between 1990 and 2012 within U.S. borders, and which caused 670 fatalities and injured 3,053 people." Perliger also found that the number of far-right attacks had jumped 400% in the first 11 years of the 21st century.

It's highly probable that the FBI drastically undercounts instances of terrorism perpetrated by right-wing extremists because of cultural double standards. As the New America Foundation's Peter Bergen has noted, attacks associated with antiabortion or white supremacist ideologies are rarely, if ever, counted as terrorist attacks. A typical example: the massacre of worshippers at a Sikh temple in Oak Creek, Wisconsin, in August 2012 by a white supremacist.

Simply put, there is an unhealthy obsession among American law enforcement agencies (and American society at large) with stopping violence perpetrated by American Muslims, one that is wholly out of line with the numbers. There is no doubt that the events of 9/11 play into this—never mind that not one hijacker was American—but there is something much darker at work here as well. It's the fear of a people, a culture, and a religion that most Americans do not understand and therefore see as alien and dangerous.

The fear of the "other" has wiggled its way into the core of another American generation.

## The Criminal Justice System

Widespread surveillance and suspicion aren't the only things American Muslims have to worry about, feel frustrated by, or fear. They can also point to the way fellow American Muslims are treated in the larger criminal justice system.

Since 9/11, the FBI has used tactics that clearly raise the issue of entrapment in arresting hundreds of Muslims inside the U.S. on terrorism-related charges. Investigative journalist Trevor Aaronson, author of *The Terror Factory: Inside the FBI's Manufactured War on Terrorism*, did the hard work of compiling and analyzing all of these cases between September 11, 2001, and August 2011. What he found was alarming.

"Of the 508 defendants, 243 had been targeted through an FBI informant, 158 had been caught in an FBI terrorism

## Surveillance by the New York City Police Department (NYPD)

The NYPD's emphasis on indicators of religiosity as hallmarks of radicalization, and on religious spaces as generators of radicalization, has put the very practice of religion at the center of the NYPD's counterterrorism policing. The perpetual and palpable scrutiny has deeply disrupted New York Muslims' ability to practice their faith. This becomes apparent in every facet of religious identity—from how one chooses to dress, to what types of religious activities one engages in, to where one prays, how one interacts with other members of his or her faith, and even what *type* of Islam American Muslims feel comfortable practicing.

*Muslim American Civil Liberties Coalition, Creating Law Enforcement Accountability & Responsibility, and Asian American Legal Defense and Education Fund, "Mapping Muslims: NYPD Spying and Its Impact on American Muslims," 2013, p. 12.*

sting, and 49 had encountered an agent provocateur. Most of the people who didn't face off against an informant weren't directly involved with terrorism at all, but were instead Category II offenders, small-time criminals with distant links to terrorists overseas. Seventy-two of these Category II offenders had been charged with making false statements, while 121 had been prosecuted for immigration violations. Of the 508 cases, I could count on one hand the number of actual terrorists ... who posed a direct and immediate threat to the United States."

Those numbers, however damning, still don't fully reflect the inequity American Muslims face within the U.S. criminal justice system when it comes to terrorism allegations. An analysis of two separate but similar cases offers a clear sense of how terrorism allegations targeting the American right and American Muslims in the criminal justice system can end with very different results. The common question running through two federal terrorism prosecutions—one against a group of seven antigovernment right-wing Christian paranoids, better known as the Hutaree militia, and the other against a Massachusetts pharmacist and Islamic radical—is what kind of speech is protected by the First Amendment and just who can rest safely under its shield?

*There is an unhealthy obsession among American law enforcement agencies . . . with stopping violence perpetrated by American Muslims.*

## A Christian Militia Case

In late March 2010, FBI raids led to the arrest of members of the Hutaree militia across the Midwest. A Christian Patriot militia, Hutaree members believed that the end of the world was near, and local, state, and federal law enforcement officers were actually "foot soldiers" in the "New World Order." According to the federal indictment, Hutaree leader David Brian Stone Sr. planned the murder of a local police officer. But that was just to be the bait. When law enforcement from across the nation attended his burial, the Hutaree would attack the funeral procession with improvised explosive devices and other homemade bombs, sparking a revolt against the government.

Seven Hutaree members were charged with at least four felonies, including seditious conspiracy and conspiracy to use weapons of mass destruction. Like many post-9/11 counterterrorism investigations, the case was built via an undercover FBI agent, primarily by using the violent, antigovernment statements some of the accused made as proof that a terrorist conspiracy existed. The defendants all filed motions for a judgment of acquittal, arguing that the government didn't have enough evidence to sustain a conviction.

In March 2012, Judge Victoria Roberts agreed with the motions of the defendants, acquitting all seven on the most serious charges. (David Stone Sr. and his son were convicted of weapons-related offenses and were sentenced to time served.) Read Roberts's decision and it's hard to disagree with her ruling, which concludes that the plot was all talk among paranoid people.

Referring to Stone Sr.'s antigovernment statements, Roberts writes, "While vile, all of this speech is protected by the First Amendment." Ultimately, Roberts concluded, the government's case was far too flimsy. "[T]he plethora of inferences the Government asks this Court to make are in excess of what the law allows," she wrote. "But the Government crosses the line from inference to pure speculation a number of times in this case. Charges built on speculation cannot be sustained."

---

*Since 9/11, the FBI has used tactics that clearly raise the issue of entrapment in arresting hundreds of Muslims inside the U.S. on terrorism-related charges.*

---

Can anyone doubt, however, that if David Stone Sr. had an Islamic-sounding name, he, his two sons, and the four other codefendants would likely be spending the rest of their lives in a federal penitentiary?

## An Islamic Radical Case

Consider the case of 29-year-old Tarek Mehanna. In April 2012, he was convicted of conspiracy to provide material support to al-Qaeda, providing material support to terrorists, conspiracy to commit murder in a foreign country, and lesser charges like lying to the FBI.

According to the federal government's case, Mehanna and two associates went to a terrorist training camp in Yemen in

2004 with the intention of later making their way to Iraq to resist the U.S. occupation of that country. Mehanna countered that he went to Yemen to study Islam and learn Arabic. Whatever Mehanna intended, we know that, in fact, he never made it to any terrorist training camp.

That, however, wasn't the alleged "crime" the FBI was most interested in. On his return from Yemen, Mehanna began translating into English and posting jihadist videos and documents on the Internet advocating that Muslims defend their lands against American imperialism. One video was particularly gruesome. It showed the mutilation of the remains of U.S. personnel in Iraq after the reported rape of an Iraqi girl by an American service member. After watching it, an associate asked Mehanna whether there was a way to try the U.S. serviceman suspected of the crime. Mehanna replied, "Who cares? Texas BBQ is the way to go."

---

*White Christians rarely have to worry that an informant or undercover agent has infiltrated their churches, their neighborhoods, or their student groups.*

---

However grotesque or cruel Mehanna's Internet activity or talk may have been, it all constituted First Amendment–protected activity. The government, however, argued that Mehanna's online activities materially supported al-Qaeda, even though Mehanna was known to have rejected al-Qaeda's worldview. He did not, among other things, believe civilians should be targeted in response to the actions of their government abroad. His belief was clear enough: "Those who fight Muslims may be fought, not those who have the same nationality as those who fight."

The distinction didn't matter. Mehanna is currently serving a 17 1/2-year sentence in a federal supermax prison. His thought crime: engaging in the same kind of violent but constitutionally protected online advocacy regularly engaged in by white supremacists and antigovernment militias on the radical right.

That, to say the least, is the benefit of the doubt American Muslims cannot take for granted in the United States more than a decade after 9/11. White Christians rarely have to worry that an informant or undercover agent has infiltrated their churches, their neighborhoods, or their student groups. They never have to fear someone watching them and taking notes. They never have to question whether the new person who seems so friendly may be just a little too friendly, just a little too provocative. They don't have to think twice before they say or post online something political, controversial, or even violently angry. None of this is their responsibility, their burden in life, just because some random person within their community lashes out in the name of God. And that's how it should be, for everyone.

# Islamic Extremism in Muslim Countries Persecutes Christians

## Spiegel Online

*In the following viewpoint,* Spiegel Online *argues that a rise in Islamic extremism in Muslim countries is leading to the persecution of Christians. The author claims that Christians are actually the most persecuted religious group in the world. Despite historical tolerance of Christians in Muslim countries, the author claims that many governments in Muslim countries tacitly approve of the current persecution of Christians.* Spiegel Online *is the online English international edition of Germany's print weekly* Der Spiegel.

As you read, consider the following questions:

1. According to the author, what percentage of Malaysians are Christians?
2. How many Christians are estimated to live in Turkey, according to the author?
3. What is the largest Christian community in the Arab world, according to the author?

Kevin Ang is cautious these days. He glances around, taking a look to the left down the long row of stores, then to the right toward the square, to check that no one is nearby.

*Spiegel Online*, "Victims of Radical Islam: Christianity's Modern-Day Martyrs," February 26, 2010. Reproduced with permission.

Only then does the church caretaker dig out his key, unlock the gate, and enter the Metro Tabernacle Church in a suburb of Kuala Lumpur.

## The Christian Minority in Malaysia

The draft of air stirs charred Bible pages. The walls are sooty and the building smells of scorched plastic. Metro Tabernacle Church was the first of 11 churches set on fire by angry Muslims—all because of one word. "Allah," Kevin Ang whispers.

It began with a question—should Christians here, like Muslims, be allowed to call their god "Allah," since they don't have any other word or language at their disposal? The Muslims claim Allah for themselves, both the word and the god, and fear that if Christians are allowed to use the same word for their own god, it could lead pious Muslims astray.

For three years there was a ban in place and the government confiscated Bibles that mentioned "Allah." Then on Dec. 31 last year [2009], Malaysia's highest court reached a decision: The Christian God could also be called Allah.

Imams protested and disgruntled citizens threw Molotov cocktails at churches. Then, on top of everything, Prime Minister Najib Razak stated that he couldn't stop people who might protest against specific developments in the country—and some took that as an invitation to violent action. First churches burned, then the other side retaliated with pigs' heads placed in front of two mosques. Sixty percent of Malaysians are Muslims and 9 percent Christians, with the rest made up by Hindus, Buddhists, and Sikhs. They managed to live together well, until now.

It's a battle over a single word, but it's also about much more than that. The conflict has to do with the question of what rights the Christian minority in Malaysia is entitled to. Even more than that, it's a question of politics. The ruling

United Malays National Organisation is losing supporters to Islamist hard-liners—and wants to win them back with religious policies.

Those policies are receiving a receptive welcome. Some of Malaysia's states interpret Sharia, the Islamic system of law and order, particularly strictly. The once liberal country is on the way to giving up freedom of religion—and what constitutes order is being defined ever more rigidly. If a Muslim woman drinks beer, she can be punished with six cane strokes. Some regions similarly forbid such things as brightly colored lipstick, thick makeup, or shoes with clattering high heels.

---

*In many countries throughout the Muslim world, religion has gained influence over governmental policy in the last two decades.*

---

## The Persecution of Christians

Not only in Malaysia, but in many countries throughout the Muslim world, religion has gained influence over governmental policy in the last two decades. The militant Islamist group Hamas controls the Gaza Strip, while Islamist militias are fighting the governments of Nigeria and the Philippines. Somalia, Afghanistan, Pakistan and Yemen have fallen to a large extent into the hands of Islamists. And where Islamists are not yet in power, secular governing parties are trying to outstrip the more religious groups in a rush to the right.

This can be seen in Egypt, Algeria, Sudan, Indonesia to some extent, and also Malaysia. Even though this Islamization often has more to do with politics than with religion, and even though it doesn't necessarily lead to the persecution of Christians, it can still be said that where Islam gains importance, freedoms for members of other faiths shrink.

There are 2.2 billion Christians around the world. The Christian nongovernmental organization Open Doors calculates that 100 million of them are being threatened or persecuted. They aren't allowed to build churches, buy Bibles or obtain jobs. That's the more harmless form of discrimination and it affects the majority of these 100 million Christians. The more brutal version sees them blackmailed, robbed, expelled, abducted or even murdered.

Bishop Margot Kaessmann, who was head of the Protestant Church in Germany before stepping down on Feb. 24, believes Christians are "the most frequently persecuted religious group globally." Germany's 22 regional churches have proclaimed this coming Sunday to be the first commemoration day for persecuted Christians. Kaessmann said she wanted to show solidarity with fellow Christians who "have great difficulty living out their beliefs freely in countries such as Indonesia, India, Iraq or Turkey."

There are counterexamples as well, of course. In Lebanon and Syria, Christians are not discriminated against, and in fact play an important role in politics and society. And the persecution of Christians is by no means the domain of fanatical Muslims alone—Christians are also imprisoned, abused and murdered in countries such as Laos, Vietnam, China and Eritrea.

## The End of Tolerance

Open Doors compiles a global "persecution index." North Korea, where tens of thousands of Christians are serving time in work camps, has topped the list for many years. North Korea is followed, though, by Iran, Saudi Arabia, Somalia, the Maldives and Afghanistan. Of the first 10 countries on the list, eight are Islamic, and almost all have Islam as their state religion.

The systematic persecution of Christians in the 20th century—by Communists in the Soviet Union and China, but also by Nazis—claimed far more lives than anything that has happened so far in the 21st century. Now, however, it is not only totalitarian regimes persecuting Christians, but also residents of Islamic states, fanatical fundamentalists, and religious sects—and often simply supposedly pious citizens.

Gone is the era of tolerance, when Christians enjoyed a large degree of religious freedom under the protection of Muslim sultans as so-called "People of the Book" while at the same time medieval Europe was banishing its Jews and Muslims from the continent or even burning them at the stake. Also gone is the heyday of Arab secularism following World War II, when Christian Arabs advanced through the ranks of politics.

As political Islam grew stronger, devout believers' aggression focused not only on corrupt local regimes, but also more and more on the ostensibly corrupting influence of Western Christians, for which local Christian minorities were held accountable. A new trend began, this time with Christians as the victims.

In Iraq, for example, Sunni terrorist groups prey specifically on people of other religions. The last Iraqi census in 1987 showed 1.4 million Christians living in the country. At the start of the American invasion in 2003, it was 550,000, and at present it is just under 400,000. Experts speak of a "creeping genocide."

---

*Gone is the era of tolerance, when Christians enjoyed a large degree of religious freedom under the protection of Muslim sultans.*

---

## The Situation in Northern Iraq

The situation in the region around the city of Mosul in northern Iraq is especially dramatic. The town of Alqosh lies high in the mountains above Mosul, Iraq's second-largest city. Bassam Bashir, 41, can see his old hometown when he looks out his window there. Mosul is only 40 kilometers (25 miles) away, but inaccessible. The city is more dangerous than Baghdad, especially for men like Bassam Bashir, a Chaldean Catholic, teacher and fugitive within his own country.

Since the day in August 2008 when a militia abducted his father from his shop, Bashir has had to fear for his and his family's lives. Police found his father's corpse two days later in the Sinaa neighborhood on the Tigris River, the body perforated with bullet holes. There was no demand for ransom. Bashir's father died for the simple reason that he was Christian.

And no one claims to have seen anything. "Of course they saw something," Bashir says. "But people in Mosul are scared out of their minds."

One week later, militiamen slit the throat of Bashir's brother Tarik like a sacrificial lamb. "I buried my brother myself," Bashir explains. Together with his wife Nafa and their two daughters, he fled to Alqosh the same day. The city is surrounded by vineyards and an armed Christian militia guards the entrance.

Bashir's family members aren't the only ones who came to Alqosh as the series of murders in Mosul continued. Sixteen Christians were killed the next week, and bombs exploded in front of churches. Men in passing cars shouted at Christians that they had a choice—leave Mosul or convert to Islam. Out of over 1,500 Christian families in the city, only 50 stayed. Bassam Bashir says he won't return until he can mourn for his father and brother in peace. Others who gave up hope entirely fled to neighboring countries like Jordan and even more to Syria.

## The Tacit Approval of the Government

In many Islamic countries, Christians are persecuted less brutally than in Iraq, but often no less effectively. In many cases, the persecution has the tacit approval of the government. In Algeria, for example, it takes the form of newspapers report-

## Views of Christians in Countries Worldwide

| Country | % Favorable 2011 |
|---|---|
| United States | 89% |
| Britain | 83% |
| Germany | 75% |
| France | 84% |
| Spain | 76% |
| Russia | 89% |
| Israel | 54% |
| Turkey | 6% |
| Egypt | 48% |
| Jordan | 57% |
| Lebanon | 96% |
| Pakistan | 16% |
| Indonesia | 52% |

Due to an administrative error, results for the Palestinian territories are not shown.
In predominantly Muslim countries, figures are for Muslims only.

TAKEN FROM: 2011 Pew Global Attitudes Survey, March–May 2011.

ing that a priest tried to convert Muslims or insulted the Prophet Mohammed—and publishing the cleric's address, in a clear call to vigilante justice. Or a public television station might broadcast programs with titles like "In the Clutches of Ignorance," which describe Christians as Satanists who convert Muslims with the help of drugs. This happened in Uzbekistan, which ranks tenth on Open Doors' "persecution index."

Blasphemy is another frequently used allegation. Insulting the core values of Islam is a punishable offense in many Islamic countries. The allegation is often used against the opposition, whether that means journalists, dissidents or Christians. Imran Masih, for example, a Christian shopkeeper in Faisalabad, Pakistan, was given a life sentence on Jan. 11, according to sections 295 A and B of Pakistan's legal code, which covers the crime of outraging religious feelings by desecrating the Koran. A neighboring shopkeeper had accused him of burning pages from the Koran. Masih says that he only burned old business records.

It's a typical case for Pakistan, where the law against blasphemy seems to invite abuse—it's an easy way for anyone to get rid of an enemy. Last year, 125 Christians were charged with blasphemy in Pakistan. Dozens of those already sentenced are on death row.

## The Persecution in Turkey

Government-tolerated persecution occurs even in Turkey, the most secular and modern country in the Muslim world, where around 110,000 Christians make up less than a quarter of 1 percent of the population—but are discriminated against nonetheless. The persecution is not as open or as brutal as what happens in neighboring Iraq, but the consequences are similar. Christians in Turkey, who numbered well over 2 million people in the 19th century, are fighting for their continued existence.

---

*Government-tolerated persecution occurs even in Turkey, the most secular and modern country in the Muslim world.*

---

It's happening in the southeast of the country, for example, in Tur Abdin, whose name means "mountain of God's servants." It's a hilly region full of fields, chalk cliffs, and centuries-old monasteries. It's home to the Syrian Orthodox Assyrians, or Aramaeans as they call themselves, members of one of the oldest Christian groups in the world. According to legend, the Three Wise Men brought the Christian belief system here from Bethlehem. The inhabitants of Tur Abdin still speak Aramaic, the language used by Jesus of Nazareth.

The world is much more familiar with the genocide committed against the Armenians by Ottoman troops in 1915 and 1916, but tens of thousands of Assyrians were also murdered during World War I. Half a million Assyrians are said to have lived in Tur Abdin at the beginning of the 20th century. Today there are barely 3,000. A Turkish district court threatened last year to appropriate the Assyrians' spiritual center, the 1,600-year-old Mor Gabriel Monastery, because the monks were believed to have acquired land unlawfully. Three neighboring Muslim villages had complained they felt discriminated against by the monastery, which houses four monks, 14 nuns, and 40 students behind its walls.

"Even if it doesn't want to admit it, Turkey has a problem with people of other faiths," says Ishok Demir, a young Swiss man with Aramaean roots, who lives with his parents near Mor Gabriel. "We don't feel safe here."

More than anything, that has to do with the permanent place Armenians, Assyrians, Greeks, Catholics and Protestants have in the country's nationalistic conspiracy theories. Those groups have always been seen as traitors, nonbelievers, spies and people who insult the Turkish nation. According to a survey carried out by the US-based Pew Research Center, 46 percent of Turks see Christianity as a violent religion. In a more recent Turkish study, 42 percent of those surveyed wouldn't accept Christians as neighbors.

The repeated murders of Christians come, then, as no surprise. In 2006, for example, a Catholic priest was shot in Trabzon on the Black Sea coast. In 2007, three Christian missionaries were murdered in Malatya, a city in eastern Turkey. The perpetrators were radical nationalists, whose ideology was a mixture of exaggerated patriotism, racism and Islam.

## The Danger of Conversion

In even graver danger than traditional Christians, however, are Muslims who have converted to Christianity. Apostasy, or the renunciation of Islam, is punishable by death according to Islamic law—and the death penalty still applies in Iran, Yemen, Afghanistan, Somalia, Mauritania, Pakistan, Qatar and Saudi Arabia.

Even in Egypt, a secular country, converts draw the government's wrath. The religion minister defended the legality of the death penalty for converts—although Egypt doesn't even have such a law—with the argument that renunciation of Islam amounts to high treason. Such sentiments drove Mohammed Hegazy, 27, a convert to the Coptic Orthodox Church, into hiding two years ago. He was the first convert in Egypt to try to have his new religion entered officially onto his state-issued identity card. When he was refused, he went public. Numerous clerics called for his death in response.

---

*Apostasy, or the renunciation of Islam, is punishable by death according to Islamic law.*

---

## The Treatment of Copts

Copts make up the largest Christian community in the Arab world and around 8 million Egyptians belong to the Coptic Church. They're barred from high government positions, diplomatic service and the military, as well as from many state benefits. Universities have quotas for Coptic students considerably lower than their actual percentage within the population.

Building new churches isn't allowed, and the old ones are falling into disrepair thanks to a lack both of money and authorization to renovate. When girls are kidnapped and forcibly converted, the police don't intervene. Thousands of pigs were also slaughtered under the pretense of confining swine flu. Naturally all were owned by Christians.

Six Copts were massacred on Jan. 6—when Copts celebrate Christmas Eve—in Nag Hammadi, a small city 80 kilometers (50 miles) north of the Valley of the Kings. Predictably, the speaker of the People's Assembly, the lower house of the Egyptian parliament, called it an "individual criminal act." When he added that the perpetrators wanted to revenge the rape of a Muslim girl by a Copt, it almost sounded like an excuse. The government seems ready to admit to crime in Egypt, but not to religious tension. Whenever clashes between religious groups occur, the government finds very secular causes behind them, such as arguments over land, revenge for crimes or personal disputes.

Nag Hammadi, with 30,000 residents, is a dusty trading town on the Nile. Even before the murders, it was a place where Christians and Muslims mistrusted one another. The two groups work together and have houses near each other, but they live, marry and die separately. Superstition is widespread and the Muslims, for example, fear they could catch the "Christian virus" by eating together with a Copt. It comes as no surprise that these murders occurred in Nag Hammadi, nor that they were followed by the country's worst religious riots in years. Christian shops and Muslim houses were set on fire, and 28 Christians and 14 Muslims were arrested.

Nag Hammadi is now sealed off, with armed security forces in black uniforms guarding roads in and out of the city. They make sure no residents leave the city and no journalists enter it.

Three presumed perpetrators have since been arrested. All of them have prior criminal records. One admitted to the crime, but then recanted, saying he had been coerced by the intelligence service. The government seems to want the affair to disappear as quickly as possible. The alleged murderers will likely be set free again as soon as the furor has blown over.

## The Possibility of Improvement

But there are also a few small indications that the situation of embattled Christians in Islamic countries could improve—

depending on the extent that nationalism and the radicalization of political Islam subsides again.

One of the contradictions of the Islamic world is that the best chances for Christians seem to crop up precisely where a major player actually comes from the political Islam camp. In Turkey it is Recep Tayyip Erdogan, a former Islamist and now the country's prime minister, who has promised Turkey's few remaining Christians more rights. He points to the history of the Ottoman Empire, in which Christians and Jews long had to pay a special tax, but in exchange, were granted freedom of religion and lived as respected fellow citizens.

---

*There are also a few small indications that the situation of embattled Christians in Islamic countries could improve.*

---

A more relaxed attitude to its minorities would certainly signify progress for Turkey.

# In Israel, Religious Extremism Threatens the Jewish State

*Isi Leibler*

*In the following viewpoint, Isi Leibler argues that the advocacy of violence by religious leaders should not be tolerated. Although Leibler contends that all speech that threatens Israel should be equally condemned, he claims that there is a worrying trend of religious fanaticism by extremist religious leaders that is the antithesis of traditional religious leadership. Leibler claims that moderate rabbis and laymen should condemn religious extremists in Israel. Leibler is a regular columnist for the* Jerusalem Post *and* Israel Hayom.

As you read, consider the following questions:

1. The author accuses Israeli law enforcement officers of applying double standards to extremist religious leaders while treating what other two groups less strictly?

2. Leibler claims that the traditional religious Zionist approach avoided using violence to promote their views, favoring instead what tactic?

3. The author accuses rabbis and Zionist members of the Israeli legislature of silence on what issue?

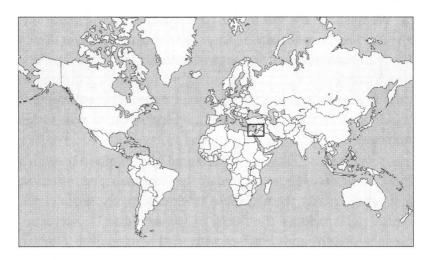

The demonstration that erupted in Jerusalem over the "arrest" of Rabbi Dov Lior, a right-wing religious nationalist leader, has the potential of developing into another major crisis. With regard to the challenges currently confronting the nation, this could not have happened at a worse time.

## An Endorsement of Extremism

Let me say at the outset that in this case, law enforcement officers utterly mishandled this issue and stand accused of applying double standards. Israeli academics have called for the boycott of their country, identified with our enemies and even endorsed harming settlers under the bogus pretext of academic freedom. Radical Israeli Arabs undermine the state as a matter of routine. Yet such acts have not led to arrests. Surely if treasonable statements do not lead to prosecution—and I believe they should—distasteful, racist and extremist rabbinical proclamations do not warrant being treated with greater severity.

Most of the nation is disgusted by the extremist outbursts by rabbinical zealots. This certainly applies to most observant Israelis who are particularly appalled and shamed when a religious leader like Rabbi Lior endorses racism and bigotry.

Needless to say, the media have a penchant for sensationalizing these issues. In this case, the central issue was Rabbi Lior's endorsement of the controversial tract *Torat Hamelech*, which suggested that killing innocent civilians in wartime to prevent Jewish casualties is a justified preventative measure. It was not, as implied by the media, a blanket incitement to kill non-Jews.

Nevertheless, most Israelis regard the manner in which these concepts were expressed to be inhuman and offensive and would expect them to be condemned by responsible rabbinical personalities—a number of whom did so. However regrettable Rabbi Lior's endorsement of this extremism may be, it surely does not place him in the same category of those endorsing acts of terror against Israelis, but Rabbi Lior was detained while the police have never acted against the latter.

*There is a worrying trend emerging on the fringes of the national religious sector.*

## A Worrying Trend

That said, if the president and the prime minister can be detained for investigation there is no reason why a rabbi cannot.

Nobody, least of all a person who is halachically [according to Jewish law] bound to observe the laws of the state, can place himself above the law even under circumstances in which the police erred and deserve condemnation for applying double standards.

The subsequent riots that took place outside the Supreme Court and the physical threats directed against deputy state prosecutor Shai Nitzan, who required special police protection after bullying from right-wing extremists, were disgusting and reflect adversely on the entire national religious community.

There is a worrying trend emerging on the fringes of the national religious sector, spearheaded by a number of extremist rabbis and religious political leaders who have decided to follow in the footsteps of their haredi [strictly Orthodox] counterparts, resorting to street violence as a vehicle to promote their views.

This is the antithesis of the traditional religious Zionist approach, which prided itself on avoiding polarization and focused rather on building bridges between the secular and religious streams of society. In contrast, the extremists are dividing the country and creating an odious image that will impact on all religious Jews and has the potential of inflicting enormous damage on Israeli society.

## The Dangers of Religious Fanaticism

Every religion has the potential for extremism and incorporates texts that can be misinterpreted. Today's Islam is dominated by the most ruthless extremists of our time, who display utter contempt towards the sanctity of human life in the name of religion.

All forms of extremism must be resisted but religious fanaticism—the belief in the entitlement to suspend the laws of society and conventional morality because one is the instrument of the Almighty—can (and has in the past) resulted in the perpetration of terrible evil.

As Jews, dispersed and persecuted for nearly 2000 years, we have good reason to identify with the downtrodden, the weak and minorities. This also encouraged us to emphasize the moral aspects of the Torah that highlight our obligation to provide hospitality and kindness to the stranger in our midst.

Alas, in our homeland, we are now witness to noisy fringe groups emerging from within the religious national framework, brainwashed by rabbinical zealots, isolated from the reality of the world and often poisoned by the hatred radiating from the Arabs surrounding them. There are some who have convinced themselves that God granted them the authority to override the laws of the land in order to promote their messianic nationalist objectives.

## The Role of Mainstream Religious Leaders

The response must be the consistent application of the rule of law to all. But the real challenge rests not with the law enforcement officials, but with mainstream religious leaders who are principally responsible for the erosion and distortion of traditional religious values.

---

*The time has come for the moderate Zionist rabbis and laymen to stand up and be counted by condemning religious extremists and marginalizing them from the mainstream.*

---

It is disgraceful that not a single rabbi or religious Zionist Knesset [national legislature of Israel] member had the courage to speak up and point out that rabbis are also subject to the law of the land. Their deafening silence alienates not only secular Israelis, but also inflicts enormous damage on the morale of the silent majority of religious Zionists who bitterly oppose such fanaticism and are totally committed to Israel as a Jewish democratic state. They are recognized as being amongst the most dedicated members of Israeli society as exemplified by their positive contribution to all areas of civic responsibility and the role they have assumed as one of the most constructive elements within the IDF [Israel Defense Forces].

The time has come for the moderate Zionist rabbis and laymen to stand up and be counted by condemning religious extremists and marginalizing them from the mainstream. This is not a question of harnessing rabbis to toe a political line. As a religious Zionist raised in the tradition of Torah im Derech Eretz (bible and moral behavior), I would certainly not entrust the spiritual welfare and education of my children or grandchildren to the likes of Rabbi Lior, who describe the murderer Baruch Goldstein as a saint. It also saddens me that a rabbi with such outlandish views can be the spiritual leader of a major community and head a hesder yeshiva.

Israel has a responsibility to ensure that any rabbi funded by the state is committed to the central values of Judaism and pledges support for a democratic Jewish state. Rabbis promoting extremism should not be entrusted to act as spiritual leaders and must be denied the opportunity of poisoning the minds of future generations.

# Worldwide, Respect for Religious Faith Can Ward Off Extremism

## *Tony Blair*

*In the following viewpoint, Tony Blair argues that in the face of current political revolutions, terrorism, and extremism, the role of religion needs to be taken seriously. Blair contends that nurturing democracy in the Middle East and North Africa means embracing freedom of religion with an open mind. Blair claims that whether or not the future is filled with religious extremism is going to be partially determined by the extent to which religion and democracy can both be embraced. Blair was prime minister of the United Kingdom from 1997 to 2007 and is founder of the Tony Blair Faith Foundation.*

As you read, consider the following questions:

1. According to Blair, what fraction of today's conflicts in the world have a predominantly religious dimension?
2. Which of the two faces of faith does Blair claim must be understood and respected?
3. What are the problems with either ignoring religious extremism or embracing secularism, according to Blair?

The term "Arab Spring" is already highly disputed. Do the revolutions across the Arab world presage the glory days of summer, or a passage through a bleak winter? One thing is certain: the influence of religion and faith in determining the outcome.

## The Importance of Religion

Consider the scale of what is now happening. Across the Middle East and North Africa, Islamist parties are ascendant. Sunni/Shia divisions are also at the fore. Terrorism, based on a perversion of religion, is disfiguring politics not only in familiar places, but also in Nigeria, Russia, Kazakhstan, the Philippines and elsewhere. More than half of the conflicts in the world today have a predominantly religious dimension.

Most (though not all) religious faiths today contain extremist groups, all capable of producing discord among previously settled communities. True, much of this extremism is based on a perversion of Islam; but such perversions of faith are also often directed *against* Muslims. In parts of Europe, Islamophobia now rivals anti-Semitism and has potent and dangerous political appeal.

In short, religion matters. Three and a half years ago, when I started a foundation dedicated to improving interfaith relations, some thought it quixotic, or plain weird: Why would a former prime minister want to do that?

I did it for a very simple reason. My experience as prime minister taught me that none of the problems of the Middle East and beyond—including Iran, Afghanistan, Pakistan, and Somalia—can be understood unless we comprehend the importance of religion. I don't mean the politics of religion, but religion as religion. We cannot treat the influence of religious faith in purely secular terms. We must address it also as a genuine issue of faith.

In fact, a fundamental foreign policy weakness, especially in the West, is the assumption that political solutions alone provide a sensible path to the future. They don't. Those who feel that their faith compels them to act in a way destructive of mutual respect must be persuaded that this is a wrong reading of their faith; otherwise, such a faith-based compulsion will always trump secular political arguments.

---

*None of the problems of the Middle East and beyond—including Iran, Afghanistan, Pakistan, and Somalia—can be understood unless we comprehend the importance of religion.*

---

## Democracy in the Middle East and North Africa

Consider the Middle East and North Africa today. Like it or not, the Muslim Brotherhood and other religious parties will possibly dominate. They are long-standing, well organized, deep rooted in communities, and, above all, highly motivated—a winning combination anywhere. Arrayed against them are the discredited politics of the old regimes and well-meaning, often numerous, but highly disorganized liberal-minded groups.

The risk we face is easy enough to describe. The challenge for these emerging democracies is to remain democratic through the traumas of comprehensive change. In particular, their economies need to reform, open up, and grow in order to meet their citizens' rising expectations.

Indeed, the region has some of the world's youngest populations, with the average age often below 30. Egypt's population was around 30 million in the 1950s; today it is 90 million. Young, aspiring populations, whose criticism of the old regime was at least as much economic as political, need their tourist industry back on its feet, their business entrepreneurs feeling confident, and eager foreign investors. They need fundamental education and welfare reforms. And the new political masters need to know that if they don't succeed, it is the right of the people to vote them out.

But democracy is not just about the free elections and the constitutional rule of the majority. It is about freedom of expression, freedom of religion, and markets that, albeit regulated, also are free and predictable. In other words, democracy is not just a system of voting, but an open-minded attitude.

That distinction—open versus closed—is as politically salient today as traditional left-right distinctions. Do we view globalization—with technology, communication, migration, and travel pushing us closer together—as something to be embraced but made to work fairly, or as a threat to our traditional way of life that must be resisted? I believe that the future belongs to the open-minded. But the closed-minded have a powerful gut appeal, and religion plays into it.

## The Two Faces of Faith

There are two faces of faith in our world today. One is seen not just in acts of religious extremism, but also in the desire of religious people to wear their faith as a badge of identity in opposition to those who are different. The other face is defined by extraordinary acts of sacrifice and compassion—for example, in caring for the sick, disabled or destitute.

One face is about service to others; the other face does not accept them. One recognizes that equal dignity should be accorded to all human beings, and seeks to build bridges of understanding between faiths. The other regards those who do not share their faith as unworthy unbelievers, and seeks to build a protective wall around it, or even to be actively hostile to "outsiders."

All over the world, this battle between the two faces of faith is being played out. What is needed are platforms of understanding, respect, and outreach in support of the open-minded view of faith.

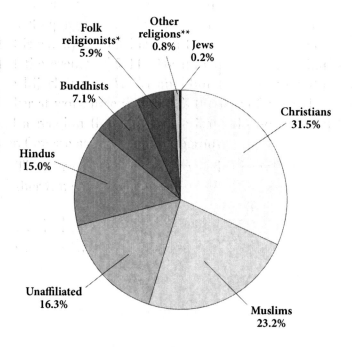

### Size of Major Religious Groups Worldwide, 2010

*Percentage of the global population*

- Folk religionists* 5.9%
- Other religions** 0.8%
- Jews 0.2%
- Buddhists 7.1%
- Christians 31.5%
- Hindus 15.0%
- Unaffiliated 16.3%
- Muslims 23.2%

\* Includes followers of African traditional religions, Chinese folk religions, Native American religions, and Australian Aboriginal religions.
\*\* Includes Bahá'ís, Jains, Sikhs, Shintoists, Taoists, followers of Tenrikyo, Wiccans, Zoroastrians, and many other faiths.
Percentages may not add to 100 due to rounding.

TAKEN FROM: Pew Research Center's Forum on Religion and Public Life, Global Religious Landscape, December 2012.

Education has a vital role to play. How many Christians know that Jesus is revered by Muslims as a prophet, or that it was through Islam that Christian thinkers in the eleventh century relearned the importance of Aristotle and Plato? And how many Muslims understand fully the Christian reformation and what it taught believers about philosophy and religion? How much do either Muslims or Christians really know of their debt to Judaism? And have we in the West any real appreciation of the true nature of the Hindu or Buddhist faith? Do we understand how Sikhism developed its extraordinary openness to all faiths, or who the Baha'is are and what they believe?

## Religion and Democracy

The point is that faith is culture; and, in today's world, people of different cultures are coming into contact as never before. Whether this produces harmony or discord depends on our frame of mind—open or closed. Can strong religious faith co-exist with such pluralism?

---

*We need religion-friendly democracy and democracy-friendly religion.*

---

This is a key question of our time. Yet many open-minded people remain curiously passive in the face of religious extremism. Sometimes we ignore it, hoping we can treat it as something other than religion. Sometimes we just give up and embrace secularism. The first ignores the essence of the problem; the second undermines faith, which still has a hugely important role to play in civilizing globalization and infusing it with spirit.

In short, we need religion-friendly democracy and democracy-friendly religion. At this time of Christian celebration [Christmas], that is an important message, of which Jesus Christ, I believe, would have approved.

# Periodical and Internet Sources Bibliography

*The following articles have been selected to supplement the diverse views presented in this chapter.*

| | |
|---|---|
| Steven A. Cook | "Egypt, Turkey, and Tunisia Are All Slowly Islamizing," *Atlantic*, May 13, 2013. |
| Jonathan Freedland | "Religious Fundamentalists Could Hold the Key to Middle East Peace," *Guardian* (UK), April 26, 2013. |
| Mohamed Ghilan | "It's Extremist Muslims, Not Islamic Extremism," Al Jazeera, June 8, 2013. |
| Shalom Hammer | "Religious Zionism or Radical Extremism?," *Jerusalem Post* (Israel), December 22, 2011. |
| Amanda Hodge | "Pakistani Christians Flee Islamic Extremists in Fear," *Australian*, August 21, 2012. |
| Daniel Huff | "Islamic Extremist Targets Facebook Users," Middle East Forum, October 29, 2010. |
| Ben Marino | "China Clampdown Hits Ramadan Celebrations," *Financial Times* (UK), July 16, 2013. |
| Haroon Moghul | "The Myth of the Murderous Muslim," Al Jazeera, January 3, 2013. |
| Yogesh Pawar | "Evangelical Christianity: Devils in High Places," *DNA* (Mumbai, India), March 27, 2011. |
| Tom Porteous | "God and Intolerance," *Los Angeles Times*, July 18, 2013. |
| Pierre Tristam | "The Greater Threat: Christian Extremism from Timothy McVeigh to Anders Breivik," Common Dreams, July 25, 2011. |

**GLOBAL**VIEWPOINTS

CHAPTER 4

# Dealing with Extremism

# In the United States, Extremism Must Be Countered at the Community Level

## White House

*In the following viewpoint, the White House under the Barack Obama administration argues that violent extremism remains a threat to the United States and that countering radicalization is best achieved by empowering local partners. The administration argues that the goal of preventing violent extremist acts within the United States requires communication and engagement with the American public, continued research on the causes of radicalization, and the promotion of American ideals. The White House communicates the official policies of the president of the United States.*

As you read, consider the following questions:

1. According to the White House, what group represents the preeminent terrorist threat to the United States?

2. The author claims that the vast majority of the federal government's engagement work relates to what kinds of issues outside the national security arena?

3. According to the White House, what are the two beliefs held by an al Qaeda–inspired terrorist?

White House, "Empowering Local Partners to Prevent Violent Extremism in the United States," August 2011, pp. 1–3, 5–7.

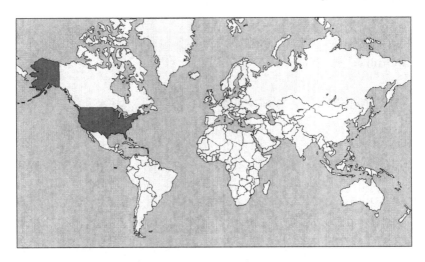

Throughout history, violent extremists—individuals who support or commit ideologically motivated violence to further political goals—have promoted messages of divisiveness and justified the killing of innocents. The United States Constitution recognizes freedom of expression, even for individuals who espouse unpopular or even hateful views. But when individuals or groups choose to further their grievances or ideologies through violence, by engaging in violence themselves or by recruiting and encouraging others to do so, it becomes the collective responsibility of the U.S. government and the American people to take a stand. In recent history, our country has faced plots by neo-Nazis and other anti-Semitic hate groups, racial supremacists, and international and domestic terrorist groups; and since the September 11 [2001] attacks, we have faced an expanded range of plots and attacks in the United States inspired or directed by al-Qa'ida and its affiliates and adherents as well as other violent extremists. Supporters of these groups and their associated ideologies come from different socioeconomic backgrounds, ethnic and religious communities, and areas of the country, making it difficult to predict where violent extremist narratives will resonate.

And as history has shown, the prevalence of particular violent extremist ideologies changes over time, and new threats will undoubtedly arise in the future.

## The Threat of Violent Extremism

We rely on our local, state, and federal law enforcement to deter individuals from using violence and to protect communities from harm. But we also must ensure that the right tools are applied at the right time to the right situation. Countering radicalization to violence is frequently best achieved by engaging and empowering individuals and groups at the local level to build resilience against violent extremism. Law enforcement plays an essential role in keeping us safe, but so too does engagement and partnership with communities.

While we can and must prioritize our efforts, our approach should be enduring and flexible enough to address a variety of current and possible future threats. Individuals from a broad array of communities and walks of life in the United States have been radicalized to support or commit acts of ideologically inspired violence. Any solution that focuses on a single, current form of violent extremism, without regard to other threats, will fail to secure our country and communities. Our threat environment is constantly evolving, which is why we must consistently revisit our priorities and ensure our domestic approach can address multiple types of violent extremism.

Today, as detailed in the *National Security Strategy* and the *National Strategy for Counterterrorism*, al-Qa'ida and its affiliates and adherents represent the preeminent terrorist threat to our country. We know that these groups are actively seeking to recruit or inspire Americans to carry out attacks against the United States, particularly as they are facing greater pressure in their safe havens abroad. The past several years have seen increased numbers of American citizens or residents inspired by al-Qa'ida's ideology and involved in terrorism. Some have traveled overseas to train or fight, while others have been involved in supporting, financing, or plotting attacks in the homeland. The number of individuals remains limited, but the fact that al-Qa'ida and its affiliates and adherents are openly and specifically inciting Americans to support or commit acts of violence—through videos, magazines, and online forums—poses an ongoing and real threat.

> *Countering radicalization to violence is frequently best achieved by engaging and empowering individuals and groups at the local level to build resilience against violent extremism.*

This type of violent extremism is a complicated challenge for the United States, not only because of the threat of attacks, but also because of its potential to divide us. Groups and individuals supporting al-Qa'ida's vision are attempting to lure Americans to terrorism in order to create support networks and facilitate attack planning, but this also has potential to create a backlash against Muslim Americans. Such a backlash would feed al-Qa'ida's propaganda that our country is anti-Muslim and at war against Islam, handing our enemies a strategic victory by turning our communities against one another; eroding our shared sense of identity as Americans; feeding terrorist recruitment abroad; and threatening our fundamental values of religious freedom and pluralism. Violent extremists prey on the disenchantment and alienation that discrimination creates, and they have a vested interest in anti-Muslim sentiment. It is for this reason that our security—preventing radicalization that leads to violence—is inextricably linked to our values: the protection of civil rights and civil liberties and the promotion of an inclusive society.

## A Community-Based Approach

The United States relies on a broad range of tools and capabilities that are essential to prevent violent extremism in the United States, emphasizing, in particular, the strength of communities as central to our approach. The best defenses against violent extremist ideologies are well-informed and equipped families, local communities, and local institutions. Their awareness of the threat and willingness to work with one another and government is part of our long history of community-based initiatives and partnerships dealing with a range of public safety challenges. Communities are best placed to recognize and confront the threat because violent extremists are targeting their children, families, and neighbors. Rather than blame particular communities, it is essential that we find ways to help them protect themselves. To do so, we must continue to ensure that all Americans understand that they are an essential part of our civic life and partners in our efforts to combat violent extremist ideologies and organizations that seek to weaken our society.

We are fortunate that our experience with community-based problem solving, local partnerships, and community-oriented policing provides a basis for addressing violent extremism as part of a broader mandate of community safety. We therefore are building our efforts to counter radicalization that leads to violence in the United States from existing structures, while creating capacity to fill gaps as we implement programs and initiatives. Rather than creating a new architecture of institutions and funding, we are utilizing successful models, increasing their scope and scale where appropriate.

---

*The best defenses against violent extremist ideologies are well-informed and equipped families, local communities, and local institutions.*

---

While communities must often lead this effort, the federal government has a significant responsibility. Our research and consultations with local stakeholders, communities, and foreign partners have underscored that the federal government's most effective role in strengthening community partnerships and preventing violent extremism is as a facilitator, convener, and source of information. The federal government will often be ill-suited to intervene in the niches of society where radicalization to violence takes place, but it can foster partnerships to support communities through its connections to local government, law enforcement, mayors' offices, the private sector, local service providers, academia, and many others who can help prevent violent extremism. Federal departments and agencies have begun expanding support to local stakeholders and practitioners who are on the ground and positioned to develop grassroots partnerships with the communities they serve.

## Goal and Areas of Priority Action

Our central goal in this effort is to prevent violent extremists and their supporters from inspiring, radicalizing, financing, or recruiting individuals or groups in the United States to commit acts of violence. The U.S. government will work tirelessly to counter support for violent extremism and to ensure that, as new violent groups and ideologies emerge, they fail to gain a foothold in our country. Achieving this aim requires that we all work together—government, communities, the private sector, the general public, and others—to develop effective programs and initiatives.

To support a community-based approach, the federal government is working to strengthen partnerships and networks among local stakeholders. There is no single issue or grievance that pushes individuals toward supporting or committing violence, and the path to violent extremism can vary considerably. As a result, it is essential that we empower local partners, who can more readily identify problems as they emerge and customize responses so that they are appropriate and effective for particular individuals, groups, and locations. To that end, we have prioritized three broad areas of action where we believe the federal government can provide value to supporting partnerships at the local level and countering violent extremism. Our work will evolve over time as we enhance partnerships and further our understanding of what tools and methods are most effective.

## The Importance of Communication and Engagement

Communication and meaningful engagement with the American public is an essential part of the federal government's work. Our open system of governance requires that we respond to inquiries; educate and share information on our programs, policies, and initiatives; and provide a platform for communities to air grievances and contribute their views on policy and government. We do this consistently in a variety of ways: We convene forums, develop brochures, respond to correspondence, post information on websites, and we make available for comment proposed regulations in the *Federal Register*. We also reach out to communities directly to answer questions and provide information and guidance, offering opportunities for communities to provide valuable suggestions about how government can be more effective and responsive in addressing their concerns. As such, engagement with local communities provides an opportunity for us to reexamine and improve how we perform our functions. For these reasons, we view effective community engagement as an essential part of good governance and an important end in itself.

---

*To support a community-based approach, the federal government is working to strengthen partnerships and networks among local stakeholders.*

---

The vast majority of our engagement work relates to issues outside the national security arena, such as jobs, education, health, and civil rights. We must ensure that in our efforts to support community-based partnerships to counter violent extremism, we remain engaged in the full range of community concerns and interests, and do not narrowly build relationships around national security issues alone. Where appropriate, we are relying on preexisting federal government engagement efforts to discuss violent extremism, ensuring that these forums continue to focus on a wide variety of issues. There are instances when the government needs to build new relationships to address security issues, but these must be predicated upon multifaceted engagement. Indeed, we refuse to limit our engagement to what we are against, because we need to support active engagement in civic and democratic life and help forge partnerships that advance what we are for, including opportunity and equal treatment for all.

Engagement is essential for supporting community-based efforts to prevent violent extremism because it allows government and communities to share information, concerns, and potential solutions. Our aims in engaging with communities to discuss violent extremism are to (1) share sound, meaningful, and timely information about the threat of radicalization to violence with a wide range of community groups and organizations, particularly those involved in public safety issues; (2) respond to community concerns about government policies and actions; and (3) better understand how we can effectively support community-based solutions.

In addition to engaging communities on a wide range of issues, the federal government is using its convening power to help build a network of individuals, groups, civil society organizations, and private sector actors to support community-based efforts to counter violent extremism. Myriad groups with tools and capabilities to counter radicalization to violence often operate in separate spheres of activity and therefore do not know one another. The federal government, with its connections to diverse networks across the country, has a unique ability to draw together the constellation of previously unconnected efforts and programs to form a more cohesive enterprise against violent extremism.

## Preventing Violent Extremism

Although we have learned a great deal about radicalization that leads to violence, we can never assume that the dynamics will remain the same. We must be vigilant in identifying, predicting, and preempting new developments. This necessitates ongoing research and analysis, as well as exchanges with individuals, communities, and government officials who work on the front lines to counter the threats we all face. In addition, we will continue to hold meetings with foreign partners to share experiences and best practices, recognizing that while not all lessons are transferable to the American context, this sharing can help us improve our approach and avoid common pitfalls.

Government and law enforcement at the local level have well-established relationships with communities, developed through years of consistent engagement, and therefore can effectively build partnerships and take action on the ground. To help facilitate local partnerships to prevent violent extremism, the federal government is building a robust training program with rigorous curriculum standards to ensure that the training that communities; local, state, and tribal governments; prison officials; and law enforcement receive is based on intelligence, research, and accurate information about how people are radicalized to accept violence, and what has worked to prevent violent extremism. Misinformation about the threat and dynamics of radicalization to violence can harm our security by sending local stakeholders in the wrong direction and unnecessarily creating tensions with potential community partners. We also are working to support and expand community-oriented policing efforts by our state, local, and tribal partners, and to assist them in enhancing cultural proficiency and other foundations for effective community engagement.

Radicalization that leads to violent extremism includes the diffusion of ideologies and narratives that feed on grievances, assign blame, and legitimize the use of violence against those deemed responsible. We must actively and aggressively counter the range of ideologies violent extremists employ to radicalize and recruit individuals by challenging justifications for violence and by actively promoting the unifying and inclusive vision of our American ideals.

---

*Misinformation about the threat and dynamics of radicalization to violence can harm our security.*

---

## Promoting American Ideals

Toward this end, we will continue to closely monitor the important role the Internet and social networking sites play in advancing violent extremist narratives. We protect our communities from a variety of online threats, such as sexual predators, by educating them about safety on the Internet, and we are using a similar approach to thwart violent extremists. We will work to empower families and communities to counter online violent extremist propaganda, which is increasingly in English and targeted at American audiences.

For example, in the case of our current priority, we must counter al-Qa'ida's propaganda that the United States is somehow at war with Islam. There is no single profile of an al-Qa'ida–inspired terrorist, but extensive investigations and research show that they all believe: (1) the United States is out to destroy Islam; and (2) this justifies violence against Americans. Al-Qa'ida and its supporters spread messages of hate, twist facts, and distort religious principles to weave together a false narrative that Muslims must attack Americans everywhere because the United States is waging a global war against Islam. While al-Qa'ida claims to be the vanguard of Islam, the overwhelming majority of its victims are Muslim.

We will challenge this propaganda through our words and deeds, defined by the very ideals of who we are as Americans.

As the president has stated repeatedly, the United States is not, and never will be, at war with Islam. Islam is part of America, a country that cherishes the active participation of all its citizens, regardless of background and belief. We live what al-Qa'ida violently rejects—religious freedom and pluralism. We have emphasized a paradigm of engagement with Muslim communities around the world, based on mutual respect and interest manifest in our new partnerships and programming to promote entrepreneurship, health, science and technology, educational exchanges, and opportunities for women.

---

*Just as our words and deeds can either fuel or counter violent ideologies abroad, so too can they here at home.*

---

But we must remember that just as our words and deeds can either fuel or counter violent ideologies abroad, so too can they here at home. Actions and statements that cast suspicion toward entire communities, promote hatred and division, and send messages to certain Americans that they are somehow less American because of their faith or how they look, reinforce violent extremist propaganda and feed the sense of disenchantment and disenfranchisement that may spur violent extremist radicalization. The federal government will work to communicate clearly about al-Qa'ida's destructive and bankrupt ideology, while dispelling myths and misperceptions that blame communities for the actions of a small number of violent extremists.

# In Europe, Promising Strategies Exist for Countering Violent Extremism

### Ralph D. Heinz and Oliver Bühring

*In the following viewpoint, Ralph D. Heinz and Oliver Bühring argue that national and local initiatives to combat extremism in the European Union have been successful and can be copied throughout Europe. Heinz and Bühring claim that efforts to counter both left-wing and right-wing extremism in Germany have been successful, as have initiatives countering extremism in Denmark, Sweden, and the Netherlands. Heinz and Bühring are former interns of the George C. Marshall European Center for Security Studies in Germany.*

As you read, consider the following questions:

1. The authors argue that the only remaining dangerous left-wing terror group still active in Europe is in what country?

2. How do several states in Germany attempt to prevent extremism in cooperation with their ministries of education, according to the authors?

3. What policy adopted by the Netherlands in the 1970s may have worsened the alienation felt by some Muslims in the country, according to Heinz and Bühring?

Ralph D. Heinz and Oliver Bühring, "A Focus on Youth: Countering Islamic, Right-Wing, and Left-Wing Extremism in Europe Means Starting at an Early Age," *per Concordiam*, vol. 4, no. 1, March 11, 2013, pp. 29–33. Reproduced by permission.

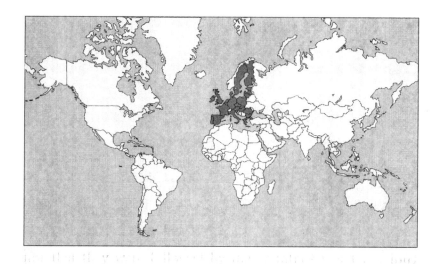

Like most countries, members of the European Union [EU] struggle with a growing number of citizens who turn to extremism, some engaging in violent extremism. The different heritage of various nations leads to different kinds of problems with all types of extremists, from left-wing, to Islamist to right-wing. The main target group for recruitment to violent extremism is young people between the ages of 13 and 30. Despite a variety of cultural backgrounds, young people are vulnerable to radicalization in similar ways.

## Radicalization in the European Union

Older theories that link lack of education to radicalization are not adequate. It is true that many violent extremists come from poor, uneducated communities with few prospects for social advancement. But there is a second kind of radical, of both the political and Islamist variety, who is highly educated and integrated into society. Both types play a role within extremist circles, with the educated being the leaders and plotters.

But even among their different intellectual backgrounds, most of the youngsters susceptible to radicalization have one thing in common: They struggle with their identity. With the various kinds of multiculturalism in Europe, it can be hard for young people to find a solid place in society. Not only are they often alienated from "mainstream society," but in some cases they are not integrated within their "own" communities represented by their parents' or grandparents' generation. Regarding ethnic minorities, the differences between first generation immigrants and their offspring born in Europe increase the sense of nonattachment. The majority of Muslims in Europe come from small towns in their country of origin. Their conservative or orthodox beliefs are challenged in the large cities of their own country, as bigger cities tend to be more liberal, no matter where on the planet. Therefore, the cultural shock for first generation immigrants is even greater. Their children, though, born in the West, are lost somewhere in between their liberal Western home and the conservative views of their parents.

---

*Most of the youngsters susceptible to radicalization have one thing in common: They struggle with their identity.*

---

Regarding right-wing extremists, the main factor is their inability to reach the social status of the parents' generation. Studies have shown that this leads to a loss of economic and social identity, which is replaced by a peer identity within radical groups. Adding to this is the uncertain economic future many young people face and their desire for strong leadership. Without visible means of climbing the social and economic ladder, young people can fall prey to a talented demagogue who addresses these problems and shows them a way into a "microsociety" in which the individual actually can do something for himself and find a useful place within his new peer group. As we will see, all prevention programs in Europe address both immediate economic issues and questions of integration into mainstream society.

# Left-Wing Extremism

The European left-wingers addressed in this [viewpoint] are more or less a homogenous group. While the experiences of right-wingers and Muslim extremists vary by locale, left-wing extremists are united by a common ideal all across Europe. And most violent left-wing extremists in Europe are not motivated by poor economic circumstances, but are part of the middle class.

Compared to the number of dangerous left-wing terror groups that operated in Europe in the 1970s and 1980s—including Germany's Red Army Faction, Italy's Red Brigades and Direct Action in France—there are very few left-wing terrorists today. Only the "17 November" group in Greece is still active; however, the Greek government does not have a special prevention program in place, but rather, treats them like any other organized crime group.

Left-wing extremist ideologies have their origin in the long-standing revolutionary Communist, Socialist and anarchist tradition of politically motivated violence and vandalism. It is an activist tradition that aims to overthrow the existing social order. The overall vision is a collectively controlled society without social and economic classes. Left-wing extremists see themselves as defenders of participatory democracy and human rights. They view current representative democracy in European states as a fake democracy without any real influence by the citizen, and their goal is to give power back to "the people."

In the leftist narrative, "the elite" use the police to suppress the common man and the media to manipulate him. Global inequality and problems imposed on poorer countries by climate change are described as the results of "Western imperialism" and "multinational companies' greed for profit." The EU, the World Bank and other international organizations are viewed as "tools of big business," and a widespread hostility toward Israel as "the extended arm of the U.S." is widely shared. There is a high level of international cooperation, and the emergence in recent years of various global anti-capitalist movements has given leftist activists a greater sense of legitimacy and motivation.

## Countering the Leftist Narrative

Efforts to counter this narrative—usually adhering to a one-on-one approach—resemble one another across Europe. Denmark uses the following steps in its successful program.

First, vulnerable young people are identified. Government programs and nongovernmental organizations (NGOs) work together with local community groups such as churches, schools and sport clubs to find kids, some as young as 12, who show openness to extreme ideas. Second, instead of lecturing the individual, police, schools, parents and other institutions engage young people collaboratively. By showing them how their behavior is seen by others using the "mirror" method ("If I witnessed the following situation, what would I think?"), community leaders try to gain their trust.

*German examples of youth counter-radicalization could serve as a model for other nations with similar challenges.*

Third, the collaboration leads to a more open discussion about motives and identities. Problems with family, friends, school or elsewhere can be addressed, and young people are shown multiple ways to solve problems. The last step is strengthening the individual's skills. Persuading a young person to leave an extremist environment is not always a realistic goal. An initial goal may be to strengthen the young person's social skills to function in society at large and handle problems and challenges in the extremist environment. If achieved, it might subsequently be possible to motivate and challenge the young person to leave the dangerous environment and find new interests. This leads to a working method that supports the efforts of the individual without condemning him (or her) from the outside. The goal is to bring the coachee to a point where he reaches the conclusion to quit on his own. Psychologists try to correct the faulty narrative that drew the person into the group, replacing his former values with an in-depth understanding of tolerance, freedom of thought and equality. The process sometimes takes half a year or longer, and includes supervision and support as the extremist withdraws gradually from the group. The concept is similar to the EXIT initiative described later in . . . this [viewpoint].

In the German state of North Rhine-Westphalia, the state Ministry of Interior, in cooperation with the Ministry of School and [Further] Education, publishes the comic series "Andi," which aims to prevent extremism by helping teachers illustrate how extremist thoughts can lead to terrible consequences. It is directed at students in the particularly sensitive age group of 12 to 18. Young people of this age are building their values and their identity. In their struggle to do so, some are misled by false idols. The "Andi" comic strip campaign, started in 2006, is a success story in Germany's efforts to counter violent radicalization among youth. Three "Andi" comics address separate topics: right-wing extremism, left-wing extremism and radical Islamist ideology. North Rhine-Westphalia developed the "Andi" comics, and afterward Hamburg and Lower Saxony adopted the curriculum, in 2009 and 2010 respectively. More than 1 million copies of "Andi" comics have been printed in Germany and demand is increasing. The comic strips are also available as free app downloads for Apple, Android and Windows Mobile. Overall, German examples of youth counter-radicalization could serve as a model for other nations with similar challenges.

In "Andi 3," the protagonist notices a friend falling under the influence of left-wing extremists and together they learn that radicalization, extremism and violence are not the solution to existing social problems. The series, with a volume each for left-wing, right-wing and Islamic extremism, enhances the ability of young people to argue in favor of democratic values.

## Right-Wing Extremism in Germany

Since Germany's first democracy was torn apart by left- and right-wing extremists in the 1930s, German officials have been alert when it comes to these threats. Since the end of World War II, Germany has established a stable and reliable democracy under the rule of law and has learned to defend those achievements against attacks from extremists of all kinds. But a series of racially motivated murders conducted by the neo-Nazi underground group NSU (Nationalsozialistischer Untergrund [the National Socialist Underground]) in the past 12 years have shown there still are frictions in combating extremist groups. Luckily, the NSU terrorists were a solitary case. Nevertheless, right-wing extremism became popular with young people in economically weak northeast Germany in the past two decades.

In modern society, schools are the center of gravity for teaching values, especially when the parents fail to provide them. Right-wing groups, for example, provide strict rules and demand discipline, which leads to strong group cohesion. Missing this in their family or school, youngsters experience a sense of belonging. The same pattern is seen in Islamist groups, especially with German converts. Many share doubled biographies.

"Andi 1," from the comic series mentioned previously, gives teachers a simple, comprehensive tool to show pupils why tolerance, democracy and the rule of law are worth defending. It is based on an everyday story describing examples of extremism in an average German secondary school. The comic stresses the importance of the German democratic constitutional state and the rule of law on the one hand and warns students about the symbols and methods of right-wing extremists on the other. By discussing values, norms and anti-democratic and extremist thinking, students can improve their judgment and explore. Its popularity is proven by the fact that other German states have adopted this comic book in their own schools. . . .

## The EXIT Initiative

In addition to prevention programs, some measures to encourage extremists to leave behind their violent pasts are also successful. Two initiatives in Sweden and one in Germany pursue the concept of helping members of the right-wing extremist scenes in those countries quit. Founded by former neo-Nazi leaders who teamed up with law enforcement, the groups EXIT Stockholm, EXIT Motala and EXIT Germany try to identify, approach, understand and change members of the violent extremist scene. To illustrate, the methods of EXIT Germany, financed by private foundations, will be explained.

The neo-Nazi scene in Germany operates quite openly and is supported by the National Democratic Party, which survived attempts to declare it illegal. For that reason, locating and approaching individuals are easier than they are with other extremists. EXIT begins with individualized coaching by psychologists. It should be noted that some neo-Nazis share ideology but are drawn more deeply into the extremist lifestyle through peer pressure and force. The EXIT initiative works mainly with those individuals who want to break from the circle of violence and criminal acts. The program consists mainly of individual psychological coaching, like that described in the section on left-wingers, and administrative support. In extremist circles, violence against "traitors" is common, so it's hard to withdraw slowly from these groups without endangering one's life. In some cases, EXIT helps with relocation, finding a job and, if former colleagues threaten retaliation, a new identity is created, similar to those provided by a witness protection program. EXIT Germany has helped more than 300 individuals in the past decade. Its success has inspired similar initiatives in the future to counter left-wing or religious extremism. . . .

---

*In addition to prevention programs, some measures to encourage extremists to leave behind their violent pasts are also successful.*

---

## The Dutch Approach to Muslim Integration

As a result of a history of Dutch colonization of Muslim countries like Indonesia, more than 900,000 Muslims live in the Netherlands, compared with 54,000 in 1971. They constitute about 5.5 percent of the population. One-half of the population of Amsterdam, the national capital, is Muslim. Muslims in the country are usually much younger than the general population, and the "non-colonial" Muslims, those mostly from Turkey and Morocco, are subject to higher unemployment rates, lower incomes and poorer prospects for social uplift. However, the number of Dutch Muslims completing higher education, including women, has improved significantly in the past decade. Muslims have also successfully established a small number of primary and secondary schools in their communities.

The Netherlands adopted a policy of multiculturalism in the 1970s and some analysts say conservative Muslims generally cannot bear the socially permissive atmosphere of this most liberal society in Western Europe. Additionally, second or third generation Muslims, who lack roots in their parents' culture and feel adrift in the Netherlands, may be attracted to extremism.

In its efforts to promote Muslim integration (which started as early as 1994), the Netherlands tried to improve the socioeconomic position of disadvantaged ethnic minorities.

Through cooperation between the government and immigrants, the objective has been to promote democratic participation, combat poverty, and prevent and counter discrimination and racism. In recent years, possibly owing to a change in society's receptiveness to immigration, the efforts were readjusted to include a newly agreed "moral obligation" of immigrants to conform to Dutch society and contribute to it. With the political changes in the country within the past few years and a right-wing party in parliament that reflects the views of a growing number of voters, integration efforts have been challenged by the extreme right of the political spectrum.

---

*In combating radicalism, the Dutch use a two-pronged approach based on prevention and watchfulness.*

---

Nevertheless, the following measures taken by the government of the Netherlands since the mid-1990s have been successful. Two Muslim broadcasting corporations and government-run television stations broadcast programs aimed at ethnic minorities. To improve law enforcement, the government has established programs aimed at increasing community trust and engagement with the police. Government money is used to fund the Moroccan "Neighborhood Fathers" project, which functions similarly to the U.S. "Community Watch" program. In both, local communities take responsibility to prevent crime and also extremism. Also, the police try to recruit employees from ethnic minorities to create a force governed by cultural diversity. Like nearly all European countries, Holland requires immigrants to take tests in the Dutch language and culture to make integration easier for the new arrivals.

In combating radicalism, the Dutch use a two-pronged approach based on prevention and watchfulness. The government tries to enable vulnerable people to resist radicalization and intervenes to identify, isolate and contain radicalization.

In this, local authorities play a key role. They promote interfaith dialogue and interethnic contacts, promoting especially sports programs. The government encourages Muslim communities to develop their own religious training programs with the goal of eliminating the need for "imported" imams who do not understand the culture and values of Dutch society. So-called street coaches, mainly kickboxers and martial arts experts who tend to be respected by young males, patrol areas of possible conflict and watch out for antisocial behavior. As another pillar of prevention, the government watches the Internet for extremist websites and has introduced its own websites to counter extremists' narratives.

The most recent problem identified by Dutch society concerns integration of minorities. The gain of momentum from right-wing parties is triggering a reaction in the form of greater Muslim extremism. The country must counter right-wing extremism more effectively to prevent this from happening. . . .

---

*It is reassuring that various national and local initiatives can be copied throughout Europe and adopted to fight one kind of extremism or another.*

---

## The Initiatives Throughout Europe

Countering violent extremism is most effective when socioeconomic gaps in the society are addressed at the same time. Faced with the obvious difficulties and costs of accomplishing that task, most countries prefer to prevent radicalization with the measures mentioned above. They can be effective, too, but they need coordinated activity between schools, local communities, law enforcement and governmental organizations. The EU is on the verge of coordinating member states' efforts and will be willing to finance programs in the very near future. Within these efforts, it's worth reminding Europe that there is a direct connection between Muslim extremism and the hostility Muslims feel in the host country from right-wing movements.

It is reassuring that various national and local initiatives can be copied throughout Europe and adopted to fight one kind of extremism or another. Understanding reasons for radicalization is the key factor, and as we can see with the Danish approach to left-wing extremism or the EXIT initiatives, listening to vulnerable individuals and building a foundation of respect before engaging in a fruitful discussion is the most promising. But the (re-) formation of a tolerant society that includes all constituent communities is equally important. Europe's long tradition of equality, freedom and democracy formed societies that acquired one special right and duty: A tolerant society must have the right not to tolerate intolerance!

# In the United Kingdom, Counterterrorism Measures Violate Civil Liberties

**Imran Awan**

*In the following viewpoint, Imran Awan argues that the government's attempts to fight radicalization through censorship and spying impinge on personal liberties. Awan claims that counterterrorism strategies that criminalize the reading and downloading of certain online materials run the risk of devastating individual lives and giving the state too much power. Awan is a senior lecturer in criminology at the Centre for Applied Criminology at Birmingham City University and coeditor of* Extremism, Counter-Terrorism and Policing.

As you read, consider the following questions:

1. Awan claims that the Tackling Extremism and Radicalisation Task Force (TERFOR) made it a priority to tackle online extremism by doing what?
2. What two laws does the author claim have created a number of controversial crimes?
3. What American counterterrorism program does the author claim should not be emulated by the British government?

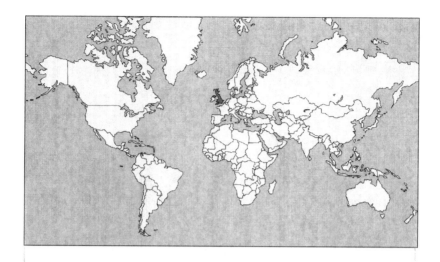

Following the tragic and horrific murder of British soldier Lee Rigby in Woolwich last month [May 2013], a number of serious questions have been raised about the UK [United Kingdom] government's Prevent strategy, which aims to reduce the likelihood of people becoming radicals, and its effectiveness in the Internet age.

## The Prevent Policy

The Woolwich murder and other recent planned acts of terrorism—in February, three men in Birmingham were convicted for plotting bomb attacks—have convinced UK policy makers that the policy needs to be strengthened.

In the wake of the Woolwich attack, British Home Secretary Theresa May told the BBC's *Andrew Marr Show* that Prevent needs to better address online radicalisation. In the case of the three men in Birmingham, evidence showed the men may have been radicalised after reading and listening to extremist material online. Prevent is currently limited to providing communities with measures to help "work together to challenge online extremism", but does not expand on the methods required to help communities do so.

A new group, the Tackling Extremism and Radicalisation Task Force (TERFOR), first met on June 3 and is currently reviewing the Prevent policy. It consists of a special committee chaired by Prime Minister David Cameron, and includes senior ministers and security personnel.

This new task force has made it a priority to tackle online radicalisation by pre-emptively censoring and taking down websites deemed to be extremist, that teach people how to make bombs or other weapons, or that feature speeches inciting racial or religious violence. (The task force will also consider banning extremist preachers from TV screens.)

## The Snoopers' Charter

Removing such websites is an exercise in futility, as they are likely to simply reappear with a different domain name.

But the government also hopes to go further, by keeping track of Internet users browsing such material, in order to prevent people like Roshonara Choudhry—who stabbed her local MP [member of Parliament], Stephen Timms, in 2010—from being radicalised over the Internet.

*There is a fine line between trying to prevent people from visiting certain websites and overly controlling access to online material.*

For instance, measures such as the Communications Data Bill, aptly nicknamed the "snoopers' charter", would allow the government the power to store details of Internet users' communications and browsing history for a year, without having to obtain a warrant. (However, a warrant would be required for the police to read the contents of emails and other communications.)

The UK government's new task force must ensure that it does not label all Muslims as potential targets, because this will only further stigmatise and marginalise Muslim communities in the UK.

Over the last 10 years, my research into online radicalisation has shown that there is a fine line between trying to prevent people from visiting certain websites and overly controlling access to online material. Such counterterrorism measures can easily become heavy-handed and impinge on our personal liberties.

The Terrorism Act (2000) and the Terrorism Act (2006), for example, have created a number of controversial offences to do with prosecuting people for downloading and publishing material deemed to be encouraging terrorism.

## The Dangers of Counterterrorism Policies

Those of us who argue that personal liberty always outweighs threats to national security are troubled by such laws. Take the case of former University of Nottingham student Rizwaan Sabir, who in 2008 downloaded an al-Qaeda training manual from the US Justice Department website, as part of his PhD research on counterterrorism. He was arrested under the Terrorism Act (2000) for downloading extremist material, and held for seven days without charge before being released.

*While terrorist attacks remain a concern, we should not give up our civil liberties for such protections.*

In 2011, Sabir was paid £20,000 ($31,280) in damages by Nottinghamshire police following his arrest, arguing that the police had violated the Race Relations Act 1976 and the Human Rights Act 1998, as well as falsely imprisoning him. The police settled before the case went to trial.

# The Prevent Strategy

The 2007 Prevent strategy was based on our understanding of radicalisation at that time. For each cause it proposed a response. The key objectives were to challenge the ideology behind violent extremism and support mainstream voices; disrupt those who promoted violent extremism and support the places where they operated; support people vulnerable to recruitment by violent extremists; increase the resilience of communities; and address grievances exploited in the radicalisation process.

With some exceptions we continue to believe that the analysis made in 2007 of the causes of radicalisation in this country was broadly correct—radicalisation is being driven by ideology, by a number of people who set out to disseminate these ideologies and by vulnerabilities in people which make them susceptible to a message of violence. Radicalisers exploit grievances; which (where al Qa'ida–inspired terrorism is concerned) include a perception of our foreign policy, the experience of Islamophobia and a broader view that the West is at war with Islam itself. These grievances may be real or perceived although none of them should provide justification for the use of terrorism. We now also know more about who is being radicalised here and about their age and socio-economic profile than we did in previous years.

*The British Crown, "Contest: The United Kingdom's Strategy for Countering Terrorism," 2011. www.gov.uk.*

Although Sabir was vindicated in the end, the case demonstrated how crudely implementing counterterrorism policies can have devastating effects on ordinary people's lives.

Accordingly, the UK government's new task force must ensure that it does not label all Muslims as potential targets, because this will only further stigmatise and marginalise Muslim communities in the UK. While terrorist attacks remain a concern, we should not give up our civil liberties for such protections. This type of Orwellian society will only lead to further unnecessary powers given to the police and the state, whose scope is already too broad and intrusive.

The British government should not seek to imitate the US National Security Agency's PRISM programme—which monitored the Internet activity of web users around the world—and ensure that any such powers under a new "snoopers' charter" are not exercised for spurious reasons. And the new task force should make clear that the golden thread that runs back to the Magna Carta—justice, due process, and the principle of habeas corpus—is not broken by these proposals.

# In the Middle East, a Good Democratic Framework Can Eliminate Extremists

## *Moataz A. Fattah*

*In the following viewpoint, Moataz A. Fattah argues that the three autocratic models used in most Muslim polities should be eliminated in favor of a democratic model based on democratic exclusion of extremist Islamists or democratic assimilation of moderate Islamists. Fattah contends that rather than viewing all Islamists as antidemocratic, the United States should find common ground with Islamists. Fattah is an associate professor of political science at Cairo University and Central Michigan University, as well as a fellow at the Institute for Social Policy and Understanding.*

As you read, consider the following questions:

1. According to Fattah, what are the three dominant autocratic models in most Muslim states?

2. The author uses the example of what Islamist organization that renounced its radical agenda through the Turkish model of democratic assimilation?

3. Fattah gives what example of innovative diplomacy that involved collaboration with moderate Islamists?

Moataz A. Fattah, "The United States and Political Islamism: From Demobilization to Deradicalization?," Institute for Social Policy and Understanding, December 2010, pp. 17–21. Reproduced by permission.

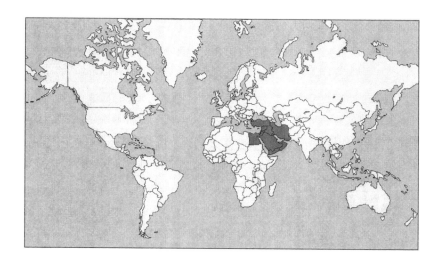

Amerian strategists fear that the transition from autocracy to democracy in the Middle East will bring Islamists to power. In other words, autocracy will give way to theocracy, even though the stated goal is democracy. The foundation of political participation is not deeply rooted in most Arab countries, and often the most organized and mobilized parties are the least liberal groups. Therefore, hasty democratization might result in the elected Islamists replacing the current fairly liberal autocracies with fairly illiberal democracies. Accordingly, promoting American-style democracy should not focus solely on elections, but on establishing the necessary constitutional framework to accommodate only those parties and individuals who are ready to endorse liberal values as stated in well-crafted constitutions.

## The Three Autocratic Models

In this regard, adherents of Washington's "principled pragmatism" should consider moving slowly away from the three dominant autocratic models in most Muslim polities, as listed below.

*Containing, but not eliminating, Islamists.* Egypt is the best example of this model, as it features both a partial assimilation and a partial elimination without clear red lines. In essence, the Muslim Brotherhood is allowed to participate in national, syndicate, and student elections, provided that it does not win a majority of votes. If (and when) this happens, election results are manipulated or else its candidates are administratively excluded from office and sometimes arrested. This model, in which "democratic" regimes secretly and selectively manipulate election results, leads to a creditability crisis and is not productive for democratic growth.

*Legal assimilation and political neutralization.* This model is best represented by Jordan, Morocco, Kuwait, and Bahrain. Islamists exist legally, but the monarch or emir has the final say as to how resources will be allocated.

---

*The [George W.] Bush administration made the strategic mistake of engaging in democracy promotion without focusing on institution design.*

---

*Autocratic exclusion.* The elimination of Islamist influence through coercion is seen in Tunisia, Syria, and Libya. Islamists in these countries are either in exile or in jail, or dead.

These three inherently autocratic models feed into the frustration Islamists hold against their national governments and the United States, which often supports them.

## The German and Turkish Models

The [George W.] Bush administration made the strategic mistake of engaging in democracy promotion without focusing on institution design. The [Barack] Obama administration can press for better-crafted democratization, models such as the German and Turkish political systems. The German formula, as expressed in the 1949 constitution of West Germany, is based on democratic exclusion so that extreme rightists (*i.e., Nazis*) and extreme leftists (*i.e., Communists*) cannot hold political office. Elections and other political freedoms are open for powers on the right and the left of the center or powers similar to them.

This model is preferable to the Islamist containment policy, since it excludes extremist parties from the political arena but allows them to enter it if they become reasonably moderate. For instance, it would force all extremists to moderate their views while enabling them to express themselves and participate in the country's political life after they moderate their views. Exclusion is only used to promote healthy democracy, not to benefit the ruling party. All political organizations enjoy the legitimate right to rule, with one caveat: no democracy for the opponents of democracy. The main objection to this model is that it is difficult to establish unless an extremist party commits a crime amounting to a national disaster or if the extremist powers are weak enough to be easily excluded from the political body. Therefore, this model might be well suited for Syria, Tunisia, and Libya, where political Islam is not a strong force; however, it would be difficult to install in countries where nonviolent Islamist movements *(e.g., Egypt's Muslim Brotherhood)* are active and enjoy a high degree of popular acceptance.

---

*The [Barack] Obama administration can (and should) strive to see more liberal democratic systems established in the Middle East.*

---

The Turkish model of democratic assimilation, which Washington holds in high regard despite some resentment due to Turkey's denial of NATO [North Atlantic Treaty Organization] and American forces to use its territory and bases to invade Iraq in 2003 and Turkey's severe criticisms of Israel's blockade of Gaza and attack against Turkish human rights activists who challenged this blockade, differs from the German model in that all parties that agree to abide by the rules of a secular and democratic state are allowed to run for office. Parties have been traditionally monitored by an institution (*i.e.,* *the National Security Council in Turkey*) dedicated to protecting supra-constitutional rules, which no party can seek to change or amend. The recent constitutional amendments of 2010 would, of course, weaken its ability to perform this monitoring role. The system's strength lies in the fact that these supra-constitutional rules guard against any individual or party that seeks to undermine democracy. The rules are not "anti-Islamist"; rather, they are standards for the whole political spectrum. Given these checks and balances, the Turkish model assumes that any political actor might try to undermine democracy once elected, and therefore ensures that Turkey as a state will continue to be democratic.

The impact of this well-crafted system on Islamist parties can already be seen. Turkey's current ruling party, the Justice and Development Party (AKP), is a prime example of an Islamist organization that renounced its radical, exclusivist Islamist agenda.

The Obama administration can (and should) strive to see more liberal democratic systems established in the Middle East. Following either model would allow the formation of balanced institutions and political systems that could be tailored to existing realities and thus help build sustainable Muslim democracies. There is, however, one caveat: Washington should not favor one group over another. It should be pro-rules and world-accepted democratic praxis.

## The Peril of Hostility

One of the greatest fears for American policy makers is that democratization will empower opponents in Muslim countries. Such logic uses a broad brush to paint all Islamists as antidemocratic and anti-Western [as Martin Kramer writes]:

> Democracy, diversity, accommodation—the fundamentalists have repudiated them all. In appealing to the masses who fill

## Proposed American Policy Based on Typology of Islamic Formations

| | Violent | Nonviolent |
|---|---|---|
| Global (in principles; local in operations) | al-Qaʿda | Al-Tahrir and the Muslim Brotherhood |
| Regional | Hezbollah (Lebanon, Syria, Iran)<br>Hamas (Gaza, Syria, Iran)<br>Taliban (Afghanistan and Pakistan) | Salafi and Shiʾa movements in the Persian Gulf area |
| Local | The Islamic Salvation Front (Algeria)<br>Jamaʾa Islamiyya (Egypt)<br>Islamist Rebels (Chechnya)<br>The Union of Islamic Courts (Somalia) | Nahdlatul Ulama (Indonesia)<br>Parti Islam Se-Malaysia<br>Yemeni Congregation for Reform, AKP (Turkey)<br>The Party of Justice and Development (Morocco) |
| US tactics | Identifying, locating, and destroying terrorist organizations and individuals | Selective engagement and deradicalization of Islamist through careful democracy promotion and peacebuilding |

TAKEN FROM: Moataz A. Fattah, "The United States and Political Islamism: From Demobilization to Deradicalization?," Institute for Social Policy and Understanding, December 2010. www.ispu.org.

their mosques, they promise, instead, to institute a regime of Islamic law, make common cause with like-minded "brethren" everywhere, and struggle against hegemony of the West and the existence of Israel. Fundamentalists have held to these principles through long periods of oppression, and will not abandon them now, at the moment of their greatest popular resonance.

---

*The United States must keep moderate Islamists in mind when crafting policy measures and should collaborate with them to achieve mutual goals.*

---

Following this logic, Washington has no incentive to facilitate the Islamists' political participation, as this would essentially amount to "helping the enemy." While it is true that most Islamist groups are opposed (at least rhetorically) to key aspects of American foreign policy, not to mention its support for Israel, close relationship with autocratic regimes, and military presence in the Middle East, it is in Washington's best interest to form strategic alliances with them. Washington must learn to differentiate between violent Islamists and pragmatic Islamists who are ready to accept compromises. The positive effects of such collaborations can already be seen in Afghanistan (Burhanuddin Rabbani and Abdul Rasul Sayyaf), Iraq (the Muslim Brotherhood), and Turkey (AKP).

The United States must keep moderate Islamists in mind when crafting policy measures and should collaborate with them to achieve mutual goals. As Shibley Telhami wrote: "Skepticism about the real aims of these groups [Islamists] should be balanced by openness to the possibility that their aims once they are in power could differ from their aims as opposition figures. This requires partial engagement, patience and a willingness to allow such movements space and time to put their goals to the test of reality." A good example of innovative diplomacy is the coalition built by President George H.W. Bush in 1990 against Iraq, when Egypt, Syria, and Saudi

Arabia participated in a grand coalition of thirty countries to liberate Kuwait. Leaving Iraq and Afghanistan and finding a just solution to the Palestinian-Israeli conflict are important steps to deradicalizing and engaging pragmatic Islamists through negotiations rather than violence.

To find common ground with Islamists, Washington can use criticisms that have been made against al-Qa'eda by other Islamists. For instance Sayyid Imam [al-Sharif], an al-Qa'eda founder and former mentor of Ayman al-Zawahiri, described the group's leaders as ignorant and arrogant, seeking personal gains, and acting against Islamic teachings.

# In Indonesia, Government Programs Have De-Radicalized Islamic Groups

*Joshua Kurlantzick*

*In the following viewpoint, Joshua Kurlantzick argues that Indonesia's success in creating a stable political system without major problems from extremist Islamists could offer lessons for other nations to follow. Kurlantzick claims that the government's policies on religion, poverty, centralization, corruption, and de-radicalization explain how the country forged a new path to success in recent years. Kurlantzick is a senior fellow for Southeast Asia at the Council on Foreign Relations and the author of* Charm Offensive: How China's Soft Power Is Transforming the World.

As you read, consider the following questions:

1. According to the author, how does Indonesia rank in size of population among the world's nations?

2. What ethnic minority in Indonesia does Kurlantzick say has been assured minority rights?

3. The author claims that other nations, especially those in the Middle East, have been reluctant to take lessons from Indonesia for what reasons?

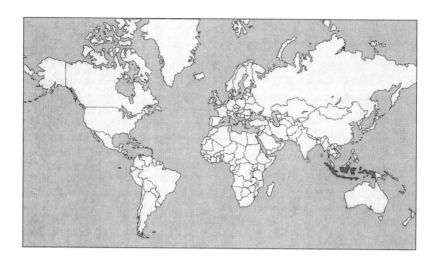

At times this summer [2009], much of the Muslim world seemed at war with itself. In Iran, protesters furious over what they viewed as a stolen election spilled into the streets and were met with a brutal security crackdown. In Pakistan, powerful Taliban-type militant groups battled the army. In neighboring Afghanistan, opposition leader Abdullah Abdullah and local tribal leaders accused President Hamid Karzai of stealing the national election.

## A Stable Political System

Farther south, the world's largest Muslim nation, Indonesia, received far less attention. Yet what happened there in July ultimately could prove far more important than the meltdowns in Afghanistan or Pakistan or Iran. Some 100 million Indonesians, spread across a vast archipelago, went to the polls, and in a free and fair vote, they reelected President Susilo Bambang Yudhoyono, leader of the secular Democratic Party. Hard-line Islamic parties fielded candidates as well, but they barely registered at the polls, gaining less of the vote than they had in the previous national election five years ago.

Yudhoyono's reelection was only the capstone of a triumphant decade for Indonesia. Despite its vast size and remote terrain—it is the world's fourth-largest nation by population, its 240 million people spread across thousands of islands between the Indian Ocean and the Pacific—Indonesia has become a rock of political stability in a turbulent region. After decades of military dictatorship, and the threat of Islamism in the late 1990s, Indonesia is today ruled by a coalition that mixes secular and moderate Islamic parties and protects minority rights. And at a time when countries from Japan to Singapore are struggling, Indonesia posted some of the strongest growth in Asia this year. The nation's occasional terrorist attacks haven't succeeded in destabilizing the government, which has steadily built a reputation for good governance and an effective battle against militant groups.

"If you want to know whether Islam, democracy, modernity and women's rights can coexist, go to Indonesia," Secretary of State Hillary Clinton said on a trip to Southeast Asia earlier this year.

---

*Indonesia is today ruled by a coalition that mixes secular and moderate Islamic parties and protects minority rights.*

---

Though Indonesian leaders themselves are hesitant to lecture other countries, their model could offer lessons for nations from Pakistan to Morocco. It has managed to create a stable political system without using its military to guarantee secular rule, as does Turkey. The militant Islamic groups that once seemed to threaten the country's future have been crushed or co-opted. And it has adopted modern antiterrorism techniques that appear to be working. In its success, Indonesia also offers the United States, constantly seeking ways to help build stable societies in the Arab-Muslim world, a model for cooperation and moderation.

# Indonesia's Problematic Past

Just a decade ago, few would have seen Indonesia as a model of any kind. The country was an economic and political basket case, riddled with graft from the era of its longtime dictator Suharto. Its heavily export-dependent economy collapsed in the Asian financial crisis of the late 1990s, plunging the country into political chaos.

Riots constantly blocked the streets of Jakarta, with many protests targeting the ethnic Chinese community. Warfare erupted in outlying provinces like Aceh, which long had wanted to secede. Hard-line Islamist groups preyed upon this unrest, promising cleaner government against the corruption of Indonesia's traditional political parties. Islamic schools, known as pesantrens and similar to madrasas, expanded to fill the void left by underfunded public schools. Some of these became notorious for promoting militant Islam, according to an analysis by the International Crisis Group, developing into feeders for the terrorist organization Jemaah Islamiah.

In the late 1990s and early 2000s, this and other expanding militant groups seemed on the verge of threatening the government's control of parts of the country, a situation similar to Afghanistan or Yemen today. In 2002, Jemaah Islamiah masterminded a bombing in Bali that killed over 200 people, and then allegedly bombed the JW Marriott hotel and the Australian embassy in Jakarta, among other sites. Indonesia seemed on the verge of disintegrating, torn apart by separatist movements and interethnic battles.

By the time of Yudhoyono's reelection, this past summer, many of these fears had vanished. The economy had recovered, the archipelago no longer appeared on the verge of fragmenting politically, and terror groups had been prosecuted and weakened. The country had held three successive free elections.

# The Causes of Success

How did Indonesia develop into a success, while countries such as Egypt, Pakistan, and Saudi Arabia still struggle just to build the fundamentals of democracy? For one, Indonesia's presidents have not allowed sharia law, the religiously derived legal system that prevails in numerous Muslim countries, to gain a foothold, except in a few isolated regions. Neighboring Malaysia, by contrast, allows several of its states to apply sharia to many issues of family law and other civil cases—a system that can alienate non-Muslim minorities, undermining the principle that democracy protects minority rights. (Recently, the Malaysian blogosphere has been fixated on the case of an Indian Hindu woman who, under sharia law, has been sentenced to caning for drinking beer.) In Indonesia, where an ethnic Chinese minority coexists warily with an ethnic Malay majority, the assurance of minority rights is critical to preventing the kind of internal violence that has racked other Muslim nations, from Pakistan (Shia vs. Sunni) to Yemen (northerners vs. southerners). Assurance of minority rights boosts the economy, too, since the ethnic Chinese, though a minority, control an outsized percentage of powerful companies in Indonesia.

> Indonesia's presidents have not allowed sharia law, the religiously derived legal system that prevails in numerous Muslim countries, to gain a foothold, except in a few isolated regions.

Unlike many other Muslim countries, Indonesia's leaders have also resisted the temptation to use the national treasury to promote their preferred version of Islam. Yudhoyono and his two predecessors, Megawati Sukarnoputri and Abdurrahman Wahid, took pains to emphasize that there was no state-preferred mosque or spiritual leader. This strategy stands in sharp contrast to Saudi Arabia, where the government plays a major role in overseeing clerics—or even to Pakistan, where former president Muhammad Zia-ul-Haq used the power and the purse of the state to institute laws consistent with sharia and pack the courts with Muslim scholars he considered allies.

Even more important, the Indonesian government has also set out to undercut the popular appeal of militancy. Rather than letting Islamic parties run on promises to improve the lives of the poor, Yudhoyono has overseen a massive national antipoverty program, increasing direct cash transfers and rice subsidies to the poor. Besides winning hearts and votes, these handouts sparked consumer spending, critical at a time when exports to the West are lagging. They also reduced poor families' dependence on Islamic boarding schools for a decent education, a point not grasped in, say, Pakistan, where politicians frequently vow to reform madrasas but spend little time investing in public education to give families other options.

Under Yudhoyono the Indonesian government also has allowed some of its power to devolve to provinces and cities throughout the archipelago, giving them greater shares of the national budget, more control over local natural resources and more money back from direct investment in their area. Devolution takes guts, especially in regions of the world accustomed to a strong, centralized government. But it also pays several rewards, reducing separatist tensions and giving average people more personal investment in the democratic process. Devolution also encourages provinces and cities to become more economically competitive.

## The Strategy Against Extremists

Yudhoyono's government has also denied the Islamists another of their biggest recruiting tools: public anger at corruption. The president has backed the national counter-corruption agency, and unlike his predecessors, has stayed out of the courts' way. Last spring, just before the presidential election, a close relative and former governor of Bank Indonesia was convicted of embezzlement and sentenced to jail time, shocking many Indonesians who were accustomed to seeing the powerful protect their relatives and inner circle.

Indonesia also has pursued a novel strategy against militant groups. The president has made a strong public case that terrorists threaten average Indonesians, not just the West. By pressing this theme, Yudhoyono has managed to turn opinion against militants while deflecting claims that he was just serving the interests of the United States. (In one poll of Indonesians by the organization Terror Free Tomorrow, 74 percent said that terrorist attacks are "never justified.") The country also has a cutting-edge "deradicalization" policy to stem the growth of militancy. Former terrorists appear on national television to describe the brutality of their crimes and express remorse for killing fellow Indonesians; former militants also approach convicted terrorists in prison, using religious arguments, compassion, and other softer tactics to win them over.

Plenty of problems remain. Conflict still erupts among Indonesia's many ethnic groups; in the province of West Papua, separatists attacked foreign workers over the summer. Despite Yudhoyono's poverty programs, much of Indonesia's population lives below the poverty line. And its military can still make trouble.

---

*Other Muslim nations are beginning to look at what Indonesia has done right.*

---

## Lessons for Other Nations

Even where they have been successful, many Indonesian leaders are reluctant to be seen as an example to other nations, especially in the Middle East. Indonesia isn't Arab, and many Arab leaders regard it as a kind of backwater in Islam, making them loath to take lessons from Jakarta. The archipelago also historically practiced a more moderate version of Islam, a religion brought by traders and mixed with local folk practices. The country's major religious organizations, with tens of millions of members, have been run by leaders committed to the separation of mosque and state.

Still, other Muslim nations are beginning to look at what Indonesia has done right. Saudi Arabia, Yemen, Egypt, and other nations have adopted deradicalization programs of their own. Clerics from across the Muslim world have descended on Indonesia to study its religious organizations and their role in society.

Indonesia's success offers lessons for the United States as well. Most importantly, it shows that Islam and democracy can mix easily, provided the government can separate mosque and state, and religious leaders are willing to go along. The resulting stability leaves far less room for militant groups, and reduces the need for the US to throw its weight behind iron-fisted military leaders like Pakistan's Pervez Musharraf just to keep militant Islam from expanding.

In addition, the example of Indonesia suggests that in many cases, America would be wise to intervene less. President Yudhoyono's counterterrorism policy succeeds in part because local people perceive the policy as run by their president, not pushed on him by any foreign powers. The US, meanwhile, has pitched in by quietly helping fund and train Indonesia's elite counterterrorism force, known as Detachment 88. But unlike in Pakistan or Yemen or the Philippines, American assistance isn't prominently covered in the press, or a flashpoint for public anger. It doesn't hurt that President [Barack] Obama spent some of his childhood in the country, and today his administration is hugely popular in Indonesia. Almost as popular, that is, as Yudhoyono's.

# Doubts Are Growing About the Effectiveness of De-Radicalization Programs

*Jason Burke*

*In the following viewpoint, Jason Burke argues that although de-radicalization programs are popular around the world, there is a growing body of research that undermines their utility. Burke claims that the research suggests that the success of the programs varies depending on local context, but that even apparent success may be explained away by other factors than the impact of the de-radicalization program. Burke is the South Asia correspondent for the* Guardian *and the* Observer *newspapers.*

As you read, consider the following questions:

1. What entity runs the de-radicalization program in Punjab, Pakistan, the author discusses?
2. In which two countries does Burke note that de-radicalization programs were well financed?
3. Burke claims that research shows that a decade after the Bali bombing, how many of the hundreds of arrested Indonesian militants are considered to be reformed?

Shahbaz Ahmed has a story to tell. It is an old story, one told by many men at many different times. It is about going to war, training, fighting in a foreign land, watching friends die and finally returning home, disillusioned by defeat.

In the case of Ahmed, however, home is a village in the eastern Pakistani province of Punjab, the foreign land is Afghanistan, the training was provided by the Taliban, the enemy was the US and their local auxiliaries, and the hardships involved a lengthy period of imprisonment in appalling conditions.

## Programmes to Deradicalise Militants

Ahmed is one of several hundred Islamic militants living in Punjab who have been enrolled in a new "deradicalisation programme" by local police. The scheme aims to ensure they do not return to extremism. The Pakistani army runs another centre, in the Swat valley near the country's western frontier, where former militants from insurgent groups spend weeks on a scheme that also tries to reverse what military and police officials call the process of "brainwashing".

Such programmes were once extremely popular. In the 10 years following the 9/11 [September 11] attacks of 2001, similar schemes were set up in almost every country where extremism became a problem, from the Far East to Europe. Some were lavishly funded, others poorly resourced. Based on classic criminal rehabilitation programmes, most involve a mix of vocational training and counselling, with a religious component designed to challenge the "single narrative" of Islamic extremism. They have been lauded by policy makers, counterterrorist experts and pundits as a critical part of the campaign to defend state and societies against militancy. The problem, however, is that nobody knows if they actually work.

The Punjab police programme, though perhaps among the least well funded, is typical of many. Ahmed, now 31, was one of thousands of young Pakistanis who went to fight US troops in Afghanistan in the autumn of 2001 and found themselves trapped by the rapid collapse of the Taliban regime. He had no previous involvement with extremism, he says, but volunteered with a group of friends from Karachi shortly after the 9/11 attacks. Inducted into a Pakistani militant group, he found himself deployed in the north of Afghanistan when US bombers, guided by CIA [Central Intelligence Agency] teams, dumped huge amounts of explosives on Taliban front lines.

---

*Most involve a mix of vocational training and counselling, with a religious component designed to challenge the "single narrative" of Islamic extremism.*

---

Interviewed in a police safe house in Lahore, he is vague about whether he actually fired a shot in anger. He does however remember how, shortly after being captured by US auxiliaries near the northern city of Kunduz, he saw friends packed into steel shipping containers. Only a quarter of them survived the trip to the makeshift prison where he was held for more than two years. More died there. Eventually, Ahmed was transferred to a prison near Kabul and then back to Pakistan, where he spent another 15 months incarcerated in appalling conditions. He was finally freed after his parents and a local cleric vouched for his good behaviour. Ahmed got married, had children and set up a small shop: "It's not much, but I get by," he says.

## The Profile of Those in the Programme

For obvious reasons, most of the deradicalisation programmes work with currently or recently detained militants. These, according to Professor Hamed El-Said, an expert in deradicalisation at the Manchester Metropolitan University, are a useful source of information, but not necessarily central to any ongoing threat. On the whole, no attempt is made to deradicalise the most committed extremists, particularly those with links to al-Qaida or who were involved in serious plots, successful or otherwise.

Why then, do Punjab police still consider men like Ahmed dangerous? The answer, police officials explain, lies in the nature of the extremism they are fighting. There have been hundreds of terrorist attacks in the province in recent years, including some of the most spectacular ever in Pakistan. Militants attacked the Sri Lankan cricket team on the way to a match in Lahore in 2009. Police facilities have been besieged.

Though there have been fewer major strikes in or around the city recently, danger remains, with "hundreds" of militants poised to move. "We are not sure why it is quiet. They seem to be waiting for something," said one senior Punjabi police officer in December. "There are lots of plans being foiled here. And lots of intelligence reports of planned operations that are called off because the militants know we are aware of them. But the capacity remains."

*Most of the deradicalisation programmes work with currently or recently detained militants.*

That capacity depends in part on people such as Ahmed, argues Mushtaq Sukhera, head of the Punjab counterterrorist police and the man behind the deradicalisation programme: "He's an ex-militant. The organisations turn to people like him for help with reconnaissance, with storing equipment, for safe houses, for transport. Without that kind of help they can't operate. It's a pattern we see again and again: people provide help on the basis of old relationships. That's why he is potentially dangerous."

## The Programme in Punjab

In Punjab almost all veterans—particularly those who fought in Afghanistan—are known to local security services. The scheme there began early last year with a batch of 300 former militants, most with similar profiles to Ahmed. It has since been rolled out across the province, from Lahore and surrounding districts where law and order is strongest, to the rougher regions in the south, where militant groups with strong links to the military-dominated security establishment are well entrenched.

Sukhera's staff, based at the new headquarters of Punjab's counterterrorist police, approached some 5,000 possible candidates, mainly aged 18 to 40 and unemployed, semi-employed or unskilled. Those who accepted received three months of paid tuition in a craft such as plumbing, carpentry or electrics, followed by an interest-free loan to set up a small business. The aim was to counter any financial offers the extremists might make in coming years.

The "students" also had lengthy sessions with religious scholars in the Deobandi tradition, the conservative strand of Islam followed by the Afghan Taliban and some Pakistani militants. The discussions covered misconceptions about Islam, attitudes to nonbelievers and less rigorous Muslims, the concept of "holy war" and attitudes to the Pakistani state: "It is a comprehensive approach," says Sukhera.

## Deradicalisation Schemes Worldwide

One of the first regimes to look at deradicalisation was the Egyptian government of Hosni Mubarak. After initial reluctance, Mubarak's intelligence services moved to exploit divisions between hard-liners and relative moderates in the Gamaat Islamiya group, which had waged a decades-long campaign of violence to establish an Islamic state. The intelligence aim was "collective deradicalisation", by which an entire group is pried away from militancy, and provided a model for later efforts.

After the 9/11 attacks, Yemen and Singapore led the way. The Yemeni scheme took the form of ad hoc outreach through interlocutors including tribal chiefs and Islamic judges. Poorly resourced and poorly thought out, it was as much aimed at deflecting US pressure from the government of President [Ali

---

# Measuring Program Success

Government-provided figures on recidivism and signed pledges are not accurate gauges for the success of de-radicalization efforts. The few success rates published by authorities cover such a short period of time as to be close to meaningless. Accurate numbers collected over a prolonged period of time may eventually offer a truer measure of achievement or failure but without a way of comparing the behavior of those who have undergone these programs with those who have not, assessing success rates becomes an unconvincing exercise.

Monitoring of parolees' associations and Internet activities may, to a degree, help determine the success of these programs, but ultimately, the primary way to measure how many detainees leave the programs still radicalized and dedicated to violence is if they resort to violence. While the limited data would indicate that the majority have not, they can continue to support jihad in other nonviolent but effective ways: Groups such as al-Qaeda will always need recruiters and fund-raisers to help run their operations. Other parolees may seek the path of "soft jihad" by engaging in frivolous lawsuits against opponents, shutting down forums for free speech and criticism, invoking hate speech laws, and working to impose Shari'a in Western nations.

*Katherine Seifert, "Can Jihadis Be Rehabilitated?,"*
*Middle East Quarterly, vol. 17, no. 2, Spring 2010.*

---

Abdullah] Saleh as fighting militancy. "There was no follow-up and al-Qaida were offering $300 a month as a salary. A lot of these guys had families to support, so they just went back,'" says El-Said. Indonesia, also under pressure from Washington but unwilling to take harsher measures, launched a programme around the same time.

The Singapore scheme, well resourced and with serious political intent behind it, seemed to indicate the way forward, and a predictably well-financed Saudi scheme was set up in 2004 when the kingdom was hit by a wave of extremist violence involving both hardened veterans of the militant training camps in Afghanistan and locally recruited men. The scheme was then expanded to deal with young men who set out to fight in Iraq and returnees from the Guantánamo Bay prison camp. Eager to show their will to fight violent extremism, Saudi authorities went to some lengths to publicise their deradicalisation efforts, hosting conferences attended by intelligence services from around the world and leaders such as [British Prime Minister] Gordon Brown who controversially shook the hands of a pair of "reformed militants" while in Riyadh. American forces imported techniques from Saudi Arabia into Iraq when they started working with the vast population of detainees in 2007–08; tactics learned there were imported to US-run detention centres in Afghanistan.

---

*One of the first regimes to look at deradicalisation was the Egyptian government of Hosni Mubarak.*

---

By the end of the last decade, as the numbers of incarcerated militants grew and as understanding deepened in Europe, the UK and the US of such populations' vulnerability to extremism, further schemes were set up. A major EU [European Union]-funded conference was held on deradicalisation in Denmark last year. Overall, there are now thousands of militants around the world in schemes with funding running into probably billions of [British] pounds.

## The Doubts About Effectiveness

More recently, however, some people are starting to ask tough questions about quite how effective such schemes are, and whether they could be providing governments with an excuse to avoid actually dealing with the causes underlying the militancy.

"Around 2009 to 2010, this was very fashionable. It really looked like the answer. Now it is looking like a bit of a fad," says Professor Peter Neumann of the International Centre for the Study of Radicalisation (ICSR) at King's College, London. He oversaw a team that in 2010 produced a comprehensive study of 15 prison-based "deradicalisation" schemes.

---

*Some people are starting to ask tough questions about quite how effective such schemes are.*

---

Those running the schemes inevitably laud their achievements. Ministry of Interior officials in Riyadh say recidivism rates for their scheme are 10% to 20%, considerably lower than those for "normal crimes". The Indonesians claim that, of around 200 militants deradicalised, only about 10% have gone back to extremist activities. The US sees the effort with Iraqi detainees as a success, though it is clear the Afghan scheme has been a major disappointment. Sukhera says none of those involved with his scheme in Punjab have reoffended and hopes to get funding for more than 1,300 militants to participate in the programme.

Recent research questions such claims, however. Both the King's College report and a comprehensive study by the RAND Corporation published in 2010 point out that recidivism rates are neither the best metrics to judge success nor particularly reliable. The Saudi scheme, despite its apparent overall efficacy, has seen several high-profile failures. (Two key members of al-Qaida in the Arabian Peninsula underwent the programme on release from Guantánamo, but then returned to militancy.) Of several hundred militants detained in Indonesia since the October 2002 Bali bombing, only 20 could be considered reformed and are actively working with police. At least 20 recidivists were involved in the terrorist network uncovered in Aceh in northwestern Indonesia in March 2010, including some who had previously been arrested for ordinary crimes, such as drugs and, in one case, murder, the RAND report notes. Equally, success in many places, such as Singapore, may be as much to do with 24/7 surveillance of the released militants as anything else, experts say. In Punjab, the former militants are all known to police and intelligence services and often have to check in regularly with the authorities.

## The Importance of Local Context

Another worry is the nature of the supposed deradicalisation. In Saudi Arabia, clerics told veterans returning from fighting US troops in Iraq in the last decade that it was not their desire to fight the unbelievers that was the problem, but their departure for war without the consent of their sovereign. This crucial theological distinction was often lost on visiting Western politicians. In Indonesia, the argument from local clerics was similar: "local jihad" was unjustifiable, whereas global jihad against "the far enemy", i.e. [that is], the West, was legitimate, given certain conditions.

"The cultural context is very important," says Philip Mudd, who spent 25 years at the CIA working on South Asia and terrorism. "The bunch of kids who want to fight in, say, Iraq have substantial sympathy." This is the key issue. Deradicalisation does not take place in a vacuum. One of the reasons for the disappointment of the ongoing US-led detainee deradicalisation programme in Afghanistan is that, when released, its subjects return directly to villages in areas where support for the Taliban insurgents is strong. "Even if you are convinced by what you have heard during the programme, you have to be a very brave man to go back to your community and start saying that everyone else is wrong," says Neumann.

Critically, Neumann's team found that deradicalisation could only work when an insurgency or an extremist movement was losing. He cites the programmes in Saudi Arabia, now almost entirely free of extremist violence, and Iraq—where Sunni militant detainees had effectively recognised they had been defeated in their multiple conflicts with the US occupying forces and the Shia population—as examples. "Deradicalisation, done well, can be extremely effective given certain conditions. But where there is an ongoing civil war, such as in Afghanistan, it is much more difficult, even impossible."

In Pakistan, where there is massive ongoing civil conflict too there is an additional complication. Many of the ex-militants on the Punjab programme belong to groups such as Lashkar-e-Taiba or sectarian outfits that have received support from the Pakistani security establishment for decades because paramilitary groups are seen as a weapon that will offset India's evident demographic and conventional military superiority.

Surveys reveal that, though those who target the Pakistani state are increasingly reviled, groups supposedly dedicated to a more international agenda or who are involved in broader social activism have retained a positive image among many Pakistanis despite the increasing violence associated with extremism, and remain deeply embedded in some communities. "We picked up a man from one village who gave us the name of literally hundreds of men in the district where he lived who were involved one way or another," one senior officer remembers.

---

*Neumann's team found that deradicalisation could only work when an insurgency or an extremist movement was losing.*

---

## The Outcomes for Participants

Sukhera, however, is a believer. Last year he spoke at length with Malik Ishaq, leader of the anti-Shia terrorist group Lashkar-e-Jhangvi and one of the most violent extremists in Pakistan. The 53-year-old militant was in Kot Lakhpat prison in Lahore with 44 cases of terrorism and murder involving at least 70 deaths registered against him.

"We had many sessions with him and spoke to him about his narrative. We defeated his logic, his rationality. We told him that this country had been created in the name of Islam and if you keep fighting, the poor of this country are the ultimate sufferers," Sukhera says. "Eventually he agreed."

The winning argument, the policeman says, was that even in Saudi Arabia the Shia are living in peace. "There is no *fatwa* against them from the Saudi clerics, so why are you killing them here, I said. We had long arguments. Ishaq is now on the right path."

Ishaq may have been less convinced than he looked. Last July he was released; there was no evidence to hold him any longer, a court decided. The number of attacks on Shia rose dramatically and in February, five days after a bombing in Pakistan killed almost 100 Shias and amid national outrage, Ishaq was jailed again.

And though Shahbaz Ahmed now says he is happily married and committed to making a success of his new electronics shop, he still turns his experiences in Afghanistan over in his mind. "I had never seen poverty like I saw in Afghanistan and I suppose it's true that with the US there and everything, there are more jobs for the Afghans," he admits. "And I never really thought that the US was against Muslims."

But many things still trouble him. He thinks, sometimes, about the problems in his own country—though he insists any effort to overcome them has to be peaceful. He remembers the men who travelled with him and the container trucks full of corpses he saw in northern Afghanistan. He, like so many Pakistanis, subscribes to conspiracy theories about the 9/11 attacks.

"What then is the reason that the [US] came so far from home, all this way to fight? Even now I don't believe the attack on the World Trade Center was the work of the *mujahideen*. It's not possible. So who did it? I don't know. I remember what I was told, how a good Muslim believes that if you kill one innocent person you kill the whole of humanity. I am sure that is right. But also that one should strive to do good and protect the weak from tyrants. I am sure that is right too. So in the end all I can say is, I don't know."

# Periodical and Internet Sources Bibliography

*The following articles have been selected to supplement the diverse views presented in this chapter.*

| | |
|---|---|
| Naureen Chowdhury Fink and Hamed El-Said | "Transforming Terrorists: Examining International Efforts to Address Violent Extremism," International Peace Institute, May 2011. |
| Robert Grenier | "Preventing Violent Extremism," Al Jazeera, August 29, 2011. |
| Andrew E. Harrod | "Silencing Speech on Islam," *American Thinker,* May 4, 2013. |
| Gerard Henderson | "Right-Wing Extremism Forces Rethink on Civil Liberties," *Sydney Morning Herald* (Australia), August 2, 2011. |
| Shelina Zahra Janmohamed | "Important to Tackle All Roots of Extremism," *National* (Abu Dhabi, UAE), June 1, 2013. |
| Cecilia Malmström | "EU vs. Extremism," *Journal EXIT-Deutschland* (Germany), October 5, 2013. |
| Pauline Neville-Jones | "It Is the Muslims Who Have to Fight Extremists," *Times* (UK), May 24, 2013. |
| Quilliam Foundation | "The Need for a Clear and Consistent National Counter-Extremism Strategy," June 4, 2013. |
| David H. Schanzer | "The Way Forward on Combating al-Qa'ida-Inspired Violent Extremism in the United States: Suggestions for the Next Administration," *Policy Brief,* October 2012. |
| Greg Sheridan | "Tall Order to Tame Extremists," *Australian,* October 13, 2011. |
| Whitney Williams | "Germany Outlaws Islamic Extremism," *World,* March 13, 2013. |

# For Further Discussion

## Chapter 1

1. Drawing on the explanation for reduced extremism in Tunisia and Egypt given by Noman Benotman and Hayden Pirkle, how might Islamic extremism in the Sahel and Horn of Africa, as described by Terje Østebø, be reduced?

2. *Spiegel Online* describes the rise in extremist attitudes in Germany as "right-wing" extremism. Drawing on at least one other author from this chapter, explain whether or not extremism is more likely to come from the political right than the political left.

## Chapter 2

1. Several authors in this chapter discuss military intervention as a cause of radicalization. If this is true, is this the only factor to be considered in determining whether to continue a particular military operation? Why or why not? Explain your answer in the context of one of the viewpoints in this chapter.

2. Among the various causes of extremism suggested in this chapter, name at least one similarity you find between the causes of extremism in different countries.

## Chapter 3

1. Tony Blair suggests that democracy must allow a place for the influence of religion. Name at least one other author in this chapter who you believe would disagree with Blair. Drawing on the author's viewpoint, make a case for this opposing view.

# Chapter 4

1. How do the programs to fight extremism in Europe, described by Ralph D. Heinz and Oliver Bühring, differ from the United Kingdom's Prevent strategy as described by Imran Awan? Could a country successfully utilize both strategies? Why or why not?

2. Joshua Kurlantzick contends that de-radicalization programs in Indonesia have been part of a successful strategy to reduce extremism. What do you think Jason Burke would say in response to Kurlantzick's claim?

# Organizations to Contact

*The editors have compiled the following list of organizations concerned with the issues debated in this book. The descriptions are derived from materials provided by the organizations. All have publications or information available for interested readers. The list was compiled on the date of publication of the present volume; the information provided here may change. Be aware that many organizations take several weeks or longer to respond to inquiries, so allow as much time as possible.*

**Africa Center for Strategic Studies (ACSS)**
National Defense University, 300 Fifth Avenue
Building 62, Fort McNair, Washington, DC   20319-5066
(202) 685-7300 • fax: (202) 685-3210
website: www.africacenter.org

The Africa Center for Strategic Studies (ACSS) is the US Department of Defense institution for strategic security studies, research, and outreach in Africa. Through programs such as Preventing Youth Radicalization in East Africa, ACSS works to strengthen the strategic capacity of African states to identify and resolve security challenges in ways that promote civil-military cooperation, respect democratic values, and safeguard human rights. ACSS has numerous research papers and reports available at its website, including "Africa and the Arab Spring: A New Era of Democratic Expectations."

**Amnesty International**
1 Easton Street, London   WC1X 0DW
  United Kingdom
(44) 20 7413 5500 • fax: (44) 20 7956 1157
website: www.amnesty.org

Amnesty International is a worldwide movement of people who campaign for internationally recognized human rights for all. Amnesty International conducts research and generates action to prevent and end grave abuses of human rights and to demand justice for those whose rights have been violated. At its website, Amnesty International has numerous publications, including "Tajikistan: Defendants Standing Trial on Extremism Charges Allegedly Tortured in Pre-Trial Detention."

## Anti-Defamation League (ADL)
823 United Nations Plaza, New York, NY   10017
(212) 885-7700
website: www.adl.org

The Anti-Defamation League (ADL) is an international organization that fights prejudice and extremism. The ADL collects, organizes, and distributes information about anti-Semitism, hate crimes, bigotry, and racism. The ADL publishes numerous reports, including "Post-9/11 Islamic Extremism in the US."

## Association for Women's Rights in Development (AWID)
215 Spadina Avenue, Suite 150, Toronto, Ontario   M5T 2C7
   Canada
(416) 594-3773 • fax: (416) 594-0330
e-mail: contact@awid.org
website: www.awid.org

The Association for Women's Rights in Development (AWID) is an international membership organization committed to achieving gender equality, sustainable development, and women's human rights. AWID aims to strengthen the voice, impact, and influence of advocates, organizations, and movements internationally to advance the rights of women. AWID has a variety of reports and briefs available at its website, including "Political Crisis in Mali and the Rise of Fundamentalisms."

## Center for Strategic and International Studies (CSIS)
1616 Rhode Island Avenue NW, Washington, DC   20036
(202) 887-0200 • fax: (202) 775-3199
website: www.csis.org

The Center for Strategic and International Studies (CSIS) is a nonprofit organization that provides strategic insights and bipartisan policy solutions to decision makers. CSIS conducts research and analysis for decision makers in government, international institutions, the private sector, and civil society. Among its many publications is the report "A Growing Terrorist Threat? Assessing 'Homegrown' Extremism in the United States."

## Global Policy Forum (GPF) Europe

Koenigstrasse 37a, Bonn   D-53115
  Germany
(49) 228 965 0510 • fax: (49) 228 963 8206
e-mail: europe@globalpolicy.org
website: www.globalpolicy.org

Global Policy Forum (GPF) Europe is a nonprofit organization, with consultative status at the United Nations (UN). The mission of GPF Europe is to monitor European policy making at the UN, promote accountability of global decisions, educate and mobilize for global citizen participation, and advocate on vital issues of international peace and justice. GPF Europe publishes policy papers, articles, and statements, including the briefing paper "'The War You Don't See': Iraq, Afghanistan and Israel/Palestine."

## Human Rights Watch (HRW)

350 Fifth Avenue, 34th Floor, New York, NY   10118-3299
(212) 290-4700
website: www.hrw.org

Human Rights Watch (HRW) is dedicated to protecting the human rights of people around the world. HRW investigates human rights abuses, educates the public, and works to change policy and practice. HRW publishes the annual "World Report" and numerous reports, including "In Religion's Name: Abuses Against Religious Minorities in Indonesia."

### Institute for Social Policy and Understanding (ISPU)
6 Parklane Boulevard, Suite 510, Dearborn, MI   48126
(800) 920-4778
e-mail: info@ispu.org
website: www.ispu.org

The Institute for Social Policy and Understanding (ISPU) is an independent, nonpartisan think tank and research organization committed to conducting objective, empirical research and analysis about American Muslims and Muslim communities around the world. ISPU disseminates its publications through a variety of channels and holds regular congressional briefings, policy events, and academic conferences. ISPU publishes articles, policy briefs, and reports, including "Facts and Fictions About Islam in Prisons: Assessing Prisoner Radicalization in Post-9/11 America."

### Middle East Forum
1500 Walnut Street, Suite 1050, Philadelphia, PA   19102
(215) 546-5406 • fax: (215) 546-5409
e-mail: info@meforum.org
website: www.meforum.org

The Middle East Forum works to promote American interests in the Middle East and to protect the US constitutional order from Middle Eastern threats. The Middle East Forum works to fight radical Islam, gain Palestinian acceptance of Israel, assert US interests vis-à-vis Saudi Arabia, develop strategies to deal with Iraq and contain Iran, and monitor the advance of Islamism in Turkey. The Middle East Forum publishes the journal *Middle East Quarterly* and publishes articles through its program Islamist Watch.

### Organisation for Economic Co-operation and Development (OECD)
2, rue André Pascal, Paris Cedex 16   75775
   France
(33) 45 24 82 00 • fax: (33) 45 24 85 00
website: www.oecd.org

The Organisation for Economic Co-operation and Development (OECD) works to improve the economic and social well-being of people around the world. The OECD is a membership organization of thirty-four advanced and emerging countries around the world that work to foster prosperity worldwide. The OECD publishes numerous studies, including "Reducing the Involvement of Youth in Armed Violence: Programming Note."

## Quilliam Foundation
PO Box 60380, London   WC1A 9AZ
   United Kingdom
(44) 207 182 7280 • fax: (44) 207 637 4944
e-mail: information@quilliamfoundation.org
website: www.quilliamfoundation.org

The Quilliam Foundation is a counter-extremism think tank set up to address the unique challenges of citizenship, identity, and belonging in a globalized world. The Quilliam Foundation aims to generate creative, informed, and inclusive discussions to counter the ideological underpinnings of terrorism while simultaneously providing evidence-based recommendations to governments for related policy measures. The Quilliam Foundation has several publications available at its website, including "The Balance of Islam in Challenging Extremism."

## Southern Poverty Law Center (SPLC)
400 Washington Avenue, Montgomery, AL   36104
(334) 956-8200
website: www.splcenter.org

The Southern Poverty Law Center (SPLC) is dedicated to fighting hate and bigotry, and to seeking justice for vulnerable members of society. The SPLC tracks the activities of hate groups and domestic terrorists across America; uses the courts and other forms of advocacy to win systemic reforms on behalf of victims of bigotry and discrimination; and provides free educational resources to teach children to reject hate, embrace diversity, and respect differences. As part of its Hate and Extremism program, the SPLC publishes the *Hatewatch Blog* and the quarterly *Intelligence Report*, as well as tracks hate groups by its regularly updated Hate Map.

### Women Without Borders

A-1070 Wien, Kirchengasse 43/13
  Germany
(49) 431 533 4551 • fax: (49) 431 533 4552
e-mail: office@women-without-borders.org
website: www.women-without-borders.org

Women Without Borders invests in women from all over the world as they strive toward inclusion and participation in all levels of the decision-making process and helps them to bring their talents and energies into the public arena. Through its global campaign SAVE—Sisters Against Violent Extremism— Women Without Borders aims to provide women with the tools for critical debate to challenge extremist thinking and to develop alternative strategies for combating the growth of global terrorism. Women Without Borders offers numerous publications about its campaigns, including the SAVE report "Indian Women Say No to Violent Extremism!"

# Bibliography of Books

Falah Abdullah al-Mdaires — *Islamic Extremism in Kuwait: From the Muslim Brotherhood to Al-Qaeda and Other Islamist Political Groups.* New York: Routledge, 2010.

Reza Aslan — *Beyond Fundamentalism: Confronting Religious Extremism in the Age of Globalization.* New York: Random House, 2010.

Imran Awan and Brian Blakemore, eds. — *Extremism, Counter-Terrorism and Policing.* Farnham, England: Ashgate, 2013.

Abdul Haqq Baker — *Extremists in Our Midst: Confronting Terror.* New York: Palgrave Macmillan, 2011.

Mia Bloom — *Bombshell: The Many Faces of Women Terrorists.* New York: Viking, 2011.

Norman L. Cigar and Stephanie E. Kramer, eds. — *Al-Qaida After Ten Years of War: A Global Perspective of Successes, Failures, and Prospects.* Quantico, VA: Marine Corps University Press, 2011.

Melissa Dearey — *Radicalization: The Life Writings of Political Prisoners.* New York: Routledge, 2010.

François Debrix and Alexander D. Barder — *Beyond Biopolitics: Theory, Violence, and Horror in World Politics.* New York: Routledge, 2011.

William M.
Downs

*Political Extremism in Democracies: Combating Intolerance.* New York: Palgrave Macmillan, 2012.

Roger Eatwell and Matthew J. Goodwin, eds.

*The New Extremism in 21st Century Britain.* New York: Routledge, 2010.

Carolin Goerzig

*Talking to Terrorists: Concessions and the Renunciation of Violence.* New York: Routledge, 2010.

Matthew J. Goodwin

*New British Fascism: Rise of the British National Party.* New York: Routledge, 2011.

Irm Haleem

*The Essence of Islamist Extremism: Recognition Through Violence, Freedom Through Death.* New York: Routledge, 2012.

Jeffry R. Halverson, H.L. Goodall, and Steven R. Corman

*Master Narratives of Islamist Extremism.* New York: Palgrave McMillan, 2011.

M. Mohibul Haque

*International Terrorism and Violence: A Human Rights Perspective.* Aligarh, India: Aligarh Muslim University Press, 2011.

Jorge Heine and Ramesh Thakur, eds.

*The Dark Side of Globalization.* New York: United Nations University Press, 2011.

Christina Hellmich and Andreas Behnke, eds.

*Knowing Al-Qaeda: The Epistemology of Terrorism.* Burlington, VT: Ashgate, 2012.

Richard Jackson and Samuel Justin Sinclair, eds. — *Contemporary Debates on Terrorism.* New York: Routledge, 2012.

Luke March — *Radical Left Parties in Europe.* New York: Routledge, 2011.

Clark McCauley and Sophia Moskalenko — *Friction: How Radicalization Happens to Them and Us.* New York: Oxford University Press, 2011.

Manus I. Midlarsky — *Origins of Political Extremism: Mass Violence in the Twentieth Century and Beyond.* New York: Cambridge University Press, 2011.

Martin A. Miller — *The Foundations of Modern Terrorism.* Cambridge, England: Cambridge University Press, 2013.

Klejda Mulaj, ed. — *Violent Non-State Actors in World Politics.* New York: Columbia University Press, 2010.

Vali Nasr — *The Rise of Islamic Capitalism: Why the New Muslim Middle Class Is the Key to Defeating Extremism.* New York: Free Press, 2010.

Kerry Noble — *Tabernacle of Hate: Seduction into Right-Wing Extremism.* Syracuse, NY: Syracuse University Press, 2010.

Jon Pahl — *Empire of Sacrifice: The Religious Origins of American Violence.* New York: New York University Press, 2010.

Angel Rabasa et al. — *Deradicalizing Islamist Extremists.* Santa Monica, CA: RAND, 2010.

Christine Sixta Rinehart — *Volatile Social Movements and the Origins of Terrorism: The Radicalization of Change.* Lanham, MD: Lexington Books, 2013.

Max Taylor, Donald Holbrook, and P.M. Currie, eds. — *Extreme Right Wing Political Violence and Terrorism.* New York: Bloomsbury, 2013.

Milan Zafirovski and Daniel G. Rodeheaver — *Modernity and Terrorism: From Anti-Modernity to Modern Global Terror.* Leiden, Netherlands: Brill, 2013.

# Index

Geographic headings and page numbers in **boldface** refer to viewpoints about that country or region.

CPSIA information can be obtained
at www.ICGtesting.com
Printed in the USA
FFOW02n2317221014
8293FF